How Household Names Began

Maurice Baren was born in Harrogate, Yorkshire. After a long career in horticulture and landscape management, he has now dedicated himself to discovering many aspects of our social history and bringing them to the notice of an increasing number of readers. His earlier titles are *How it All Began*, his first book about the history behind certain brand names, *How it All Began in the Garden*, the stories behind plant names and the people who collected plants or grew them in their nurseries and gardens, and, in 1996, *How it All Began Up the High Street*, the stories behind the shop fronts.

How Household Names Began

Maurice Baren

Special Edition for PAST TIMES® Oxford, England

First published in Great Britain in 1997 by
Michael O'Mara Books Limited
9 Lion Yard, Tremadoc Road
London SW4 7NQ

A CIP catalogue record of this book is available from the British Library

ISBN 1-85479-257-1

3 5 7 9 10 8 6 4 2

Designed and typeset by Martin Bristow

Printed and bound in Italy
by L.E.G.O., Vicenza

Contents

Author's Note

I would like to record my thanks to those who have helped me to complete this, my fourth book. I am particularly grateful to all the companies who are featured in the book, those people who have loaned me illustrations and other authors who have allowed me to use their research material. I would like to thank the following for their special help with pictures: Nadine Meisner, Francis Spear, Philip Haythornwaite and Professor Michael Harvey. Additionally, I would very much like to thank Dr Fred Kidd, Tom and Peggy Hewitt, John Hopkinson, the late Dr Alan Walker, Glasgow Library, Sandra Volb, and the staff of Michael O'Mara Books, particularly Lesley O'Mara and Annabel Reid, for their kindnesss, help and support.

I do apologize if anyone feels I have failed to give them credit. It has not been done intentionally and I will try and make amends in future editions.

Throughout the compilation of this book, its research, writing and gathering of illustrative material, my wife, Judith, has been a tremendous help and, in thanking her for her continued love and support, I dedicate it to her.

Bibliography

BEABLE, W H, *Romance of Great Businesses*, Heath Cranton, 1926

BEAVER, PATRICK, *The Matchmakers*, Henry Melland, 1985

GREEN, DAVID, *CPC (United Kingdom): A History*, Publications for Companies, 1979

GRENVILLE SMITH, R and ALEXANDER BARRIE, *Aspro: How a Family Business Grew Up*, Nicholas International Ltd, 1976

HARVEY, MICHAEL, *Patons: A Story of Handknitting*, Springwood Books, 1985

HUNT, JONATHAN, *Pinmakers to the World*, James & James, 1985

KAVLI: *Presentasjon av en jubilant*, Kavli

REGER, JANET with SHIRLEY FLACK, *Janet Reger: Her Story*, Chapmans, 1991

MORITA, AKIO and THE SONY CORPORATION, *Made in Japan*, HarperCollins Publishers, 1987

Introduction

It has been good to receive so many appreciative comments about *How it All Began* and its successors *How it All Began in the Garden* and *How it All Began Up the High Street*. I have therefore been encouraged to compile a sequel to my first book and here we have a further selection of brand names and the fascinating stories behind these products.

We start with Aga, a well-known name in cookers, particularly among those who live in rural areas – and almost a cult item for many who live in towns. Did you know that its inventor developed special beacons for Scandinavian lighthouses before he created a cooker for his wife's kitchen? We end with Yardley of London, which was started by one William Yardley, a sword cutler of Bloomsbury.

How do brand names, such as Sony, Ty-Phoo or UHU, come into existence? Read on and you'll find the answers. The choice of name can be so important to the success of a product: Tokyo Tsushin Kogyo Kabushiki Kaisha nearly slipped up in their choice, but chose Sony. Barking dogs can be painful to the ear, aching feet can also hurt, but Hush Puppies were named after balls of dough – find the link in the book! A company who initially made illuminated walking sticks for night travellers and glowing magicians' wands took a simple phrase 'Ever Ready' for its trading name.

Once again, almost every page of this book contains old advertisements, some dating back to before the turn of the century, and there are many previously unpublished photographs and other illustrations. This is another dipping-into book, a source book for those family quizzes or for useful information when the children are completing school projects. It is an ideal gift book for that favourite aunt or uncle who has everything or for that friend who revels in nostalgia. To all who enjoy the *How it All Began* series – happy reading. May it fire your own curiosity about what is behind the commonplace.

Maurice Baren 1997

Gustaf Dalén was born into a peasant family, on a farm in Sweden in 1869. As a boy he disliked doing chores on the farm, much preferring to try inventing things. His first creation used an old spinning wheel to produce power to shell dried beans for the family's winter supply. Next, he developed a device that would not only wake him up in the morning but would also make him a cup of coffee. He used an old clock to rotate a spool at a pre-set time; the spool ignited a match which, using a series of cords and levers, lit an oil lamp. A coffee pot hung over the lamp flame, and in fifteen minutes a hammer started beating against an iron plate – Gustaf was woken up, the room was lit and coffee was ready!

When he was twenty-three, Gustaf left the farm to train as an engineer with De Laval, the inventor of the cream separator. Aware of Sweden's rugged coastline with its need for many lighthouses, Gustaf soon turned his mind to creating an automatic beacon to reduce the costs of running the lighthouse service. Later, he also invented a sun valve which cut off the gas supply when daylight levels were sufficient for ships to pass along the coastline safely.

Gustaf's inventions won him great acclaim and he was granted the contract to light the Panama Canal. However, in 1912, when carrying out an experiment, some materials exploded and he lost his sight. Although he was awarded the Swedish Royal Academy of Science Nobel Prize in Physics he was saddened because he felt useless. He did not allow these feelings to last long, however, and he soon resumed his duties as president of the AGA acetylene company (Aktiebolaget Gas Accumulator).

"You know, dear, I think my Aga has been alight since the last Coronation."

During his recuperation from the accident, Gustaf became aware of the difficulties his wife was having with a cast iron cooking grate. It was temperamental and the temperature fluctuated so much that it needed constant supervision. Putting his inventive skills to work, he created a cooker which needed no gauges and only the minimum of supervision, the Aga.

The Aga works on the principle of heat storage and uses only a small amount of energy, the heat being stored in the iron castings inside the cooker. To retain the heat the

Aga is highly insulated so that set temperatures can be easily maintained; it also has an automatic thermostatic control. The Aga has two large insulating lids which when lowered retain the heat, and when raised reveal the boiling and simmering plates.

In 1936, the sixty-seven-year-old president of AGA called a meeting of his Board of Directors and said, 'My doctor tells me that I have a cancer which cannot be cured. I shall go on as long as possible.' He then moved to the next item of business.

Gustaf Dalén died in his villa overlooking the harbour on 9 December 1937, and as the ships passed through the channel that dark December day they reduced speed and lowered their flags in mourning for the man who had enabled them to be guided safely home. Today his name may be little known, but his cooker is appreciated in many, many thousands of kitchens.

FACING PAGE, TOP: *Gustaf Dalén*
FACING PAGE, BELOW: *Part of a 1953 advertisement*
ABOVE: *Cartoon in* Punch, *1953*
RIGHT: *A modern Aga kitchen*

Andrews
SALTS

William Henry Scott was a margarine importer and commission agent. In 1885, he and William Turner Murdoch, a provision agent, operated from the same building in White Hart Yard, in the old part of Newcastle upon Tyne.

Over the next ten years they amalgamated and leased No. 4 Gallowgate, premises opposite the tiny eleventh-century St Andrew's Church. As provision importers they would deal with all the ingredients of liver salt, but how they came across the formula is a mystery.

Andrews Liver Salt, taking its name from the church, was sold as an effective remedy for indigestion, headache, biliousness, constipation, liver and kidney disorders and rheumatism! It was originally sold in 5-lb sweet jars, and then dispensed in 1d and ½d twists (a paper bag 'twisted' from small pieces of flat paper) to miners and sailors who visited Newcastle. Prior to 1909, Andrews was sold in glass bottles but then, due to difficulties caused by dampness and breakages, the famous tins appeared.

Andrews pioneered the branding and advertising of products and by the 1920s already used coupons, gift schemes and competitions. Customers

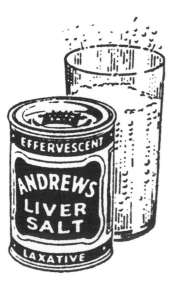

A glass of **Andrews** in the morning makes you feel *Fine!*

STANDARD SIZE 1/10d · FAMILY SIZE 2/10d

THE IMPORTANCE OF INNER CLEANLINESS

Sparkling Andrews refreshes the mouth and helps to clean the tongue.

Effervescent Andrews is antacid; soothes your stomach; corrects digestive upsets; tones up the liver and checks biliousness.

Pleasant-tasting Andrews gently clears the system, thus promoting inner cleanliness.

were encouraged to save the lids from tins and in return might win a prize of £15, a gold watch, scissors, fountain pens, silver thimbles, butter dishes, tooth-brushes, playing cards or Andrews 'Happy Family' cards. It was estimated that in the 1920s an Andrews advertisement reached every person in the United Kingdom at least once a week; Andrews had the largest sale of any similar product. Between the two World Wars people became more interested in the

other home in Britain had a tin in the cupboard. There was a 96 per cent consumer awareness and a very high brand loyalty.

The company became Phillips, Scott and Turner and sold Phillips Milk of Magnesia, but changed its name to Sterling Health in 1972. In 1995, when Sterling Health ceased trading, the product was taken over by SmithKline Beecham.

FACING PAGE, TOP: *Advertisement in* John Bull. *1956*
LEFT: *Advertisement from the 1940s*
BELOW: *Showcard from the 1940s*

"I must have left it behind!"

Andrews

LIVER SALT

for a Merry Christmas
the day after

open air and Andrews advertisements reflected this with slogans such as Andrews 'keeps you fit', 'wards off the ills of life' and eventually the most famous one: 'Andrews for inner cleanliness'.

During the Second World War, Andrews was still produced, but was packed in treated cardboard containers. By 1950, UK sales had levelled out. However, export sales grew and tins were printed in eighteen languages. At that time it was said that every

FOR FAMILY HEALTH—
Inner Cleanliness Comes First!

＼ANGLEPOISE＼

George Carwardine was born in Bath in 1887, the second youngest of twelve surviving children. He won a scholarship to the Bath Bluecoat School, but left when he was fourteen. As a young man he studied to become a minister, hoping to join his brother, Charles, a missionary in China, but ill health prevented him doing so. From 1901–5, George was an apprentice at the Whiting Auto Works and was subsequently employed in several engineering workshops in Bath.

In 1912, he started as a chargehand at the Horstmann Car Company; by 1916 he was both works manager and chief designer, being largely responsible for the design of all their cars.

George Carwardine started his own business, Cardine Accessories, in 1924 in Locksbrook Road, Bath, designing and manufacturing various items, but primarily automobile suspension systems. His interest

in springs, weights and sliding mechanisms led him to develop apparatus which could move through three planes, but hold still in any given position. However, at that time he was in demand by the motor industry and this project had to be put to one side.

Cardine Accessories ceased operations in the late 1920s. George became a freelance consulting engineer and inventor and at last he saw his opportunity: the aim of his previous work was to create a lamp – it would have a frictionless mechanism which could balance and direct the light of an incandescent bulb to any position in three planes. The lamp would have the same versatility of

LEFT: *George Carwardine*
ABOVE: *The original Anglepoise lamp, 1933*
FACING PAGE, TOP: *Advertisement in* Punch, *1949*
FACING PAGE, BELOW: *The Artikula task lamp's unique jointing mechanism is based on the human spine*

movement as the human arm – instant flexibility, the ability to hold a chosen position – and all at the touch of a finger. Turning the theory into reality must have been a formidable task involving complex mathematical calculations, and with no help from computers or calculators.

The original United Kingdom patent for the 'Equipoise' stated that the desired result could be achieved in a number of ways, the most satisfactory being to use 'equipoising springs'. These springs had to be twisted tightly and were therefore difficult to manufacture, so he approached Herbert Terry & Sons, renowned spring manufacturers of Redditch, a company he knew well.

They worked together and, in 1932, a patent for 'Improvements in Elastic Equipoising Mechanisms' was filed. The name 'Equipoise' could not be registered as a trademark as it already existed in the English language – a new word was needed and 'Anglepoise' was coined. It is now the vigorously protected trade name of Anglepoise Ltd.

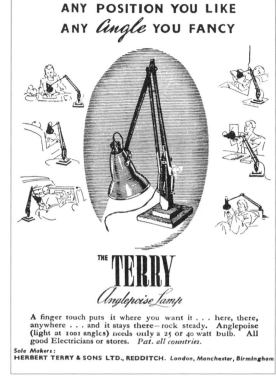

ANY POSITION YOU LIKE
ANY *Angle* YOU FANCY

THE **TERRY**
Anglepoise Lamp

A finger touch puts it where you want it . . . here, there, anywhere . . . and it stays there—rock steady. Anglepoise (light at 1001 angles) needs only a 25 or 40 watt bulb. All good Electricians or stores. *Pat. all countries.*

Sole Makers:
HERBERT TERRY & SONS LTD., REDDITCH. London, Manchester, Birmingham

It was originally envisaged that the lamp would be used in industrial, and a few commercial, applications, but it quickly became evident that it could be marketed for use in the home and office. The result was to become a design icon: Model 1227, the classic Anglepoise.

It was a lamp that was engineered rather than designed, and has been likened to Issigonis's Mini – both have been described as unstyled, but strangely appealing, possessing that certain something!

Terry's purchased the licence to become the exclusive manufacturers

and paid Carwardine a royalty based on production figures. George produced 'bespoke' designs for 'angle-poising' lights for use in operating theatres, hospital wards and by the Post Office to name but a few; similarly he helped develop stands for microphones, loudspeakers and mirrors.

In many countries patent protection was secured. In Norway, Jac Jacobsen initially became Scandinavian agent for Anglepoise products, and later started manufacturing them under licence, naming his company Luxo. Charles Terry permitted Jacobsen to enter the United States market, and, after the US patent ran

Anglepoise
the lamp with the personal touch

out in 1953, Luxo's American operation reached a turnover of \$1 million in eight years. Today Luxo is a major world-wide company.

Meanwhile, back in Britain, Terry's continued to produce Anglepoise lamps, along with products ranging from chest expanders to expandable arm-bands. In 1971, Terry's was bought by the world's largest spring makers, the United States giant Associated Spring Corporation and John Terry, the founder's grandson, remained as managing director. The production of Anglepoise lamps continued, but the new company showed little interest in that part of the venture, wishing to concentrate on the manufacture and sale of springs. This seemed a shame to John and, in 1975, he and his cousin Ray, who was managing director of his own lighting company, bought from Associated Spring everything to do with Anglepoise. The plant and stock was transferred in its entirety, over a single weekend, from the old Terry works to a new factory.

Once again Anglepoise is a small family business; once again it is an innovative company. In 1994, its 'Artikula' light, a product of British design and manufacture, was featured at the Science Museum in London just weeks after its official launch. Another area in which Anglepoise is working is in providing appropriate lights for those who are partially sighted, a group of people who have particular needs, often met by using a compact fluorescent luminaire.

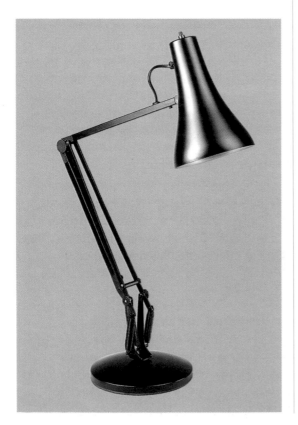

ABOVE: *1968 advertisement*
LEFT: *Limited edition to celebrate sixty years of Anglepoise*

FACING PAGE, TOP: *Advertisement in* Vogue, *1953*
FACING PAGE, BELOW: *Advertisement in* Vogue, c. *1926*

Back in the days of Elizabeth I, in 1586, William Lee, a poor parish priest in Calverton, Nottinghamshire, invented the first knitting machine. Although he died in poverty, his invention lived on and the hand-frame knitting of stockings became a cottage industry in the Nottingham area. In 1864, William Cotton of Loughborough devised a method of machine-knitting fabric whereby it could be shaped or fashioned automatically, and all machines which embody this principle are known as 'Cotton's Patent'.

For this year of elegance

THE ARISTOCRAT OF STOCKINGS

Early in this century most British women were limited to factory-produced, coarse-gauge wool or cotton stockings, available in black or white – neither being glamorous! However, if grandmama had the money, she could have a pair of pure silk, fine-gauge stockings made by a 'stockinger' on a machine he kept in an upstairs room of his cottage.

After the First World War, American women could buy full-fashioned pure silk 39-gauge stockings at affordable prices.

In England sixteen-year-old Albert Ernest Allen joined his uncle, a small hosiery manufacturer, in Nottingham. By the age of forty-one he had become a director of Robert Rowley & Co Ltd at Leicester, one of the largest hosiery companies in the country. He specialized in selling, having picked up all his technical knowledge through years of handling the merchandise.

He was interested in developing a silk hosiery industry in this country and, in 1919, he resigned from Rowley's and sailed for the United States to see how they made silk stockings. On his return, with only £500 savings but with the help of friends, he built a factory at Langley Mill, just northwest of Nottingham. In the village were old cottages, each with its 'stockinger's window', which had been specially shaped to throw light on to the old handframe and there was still a reservoir of skilled labour able to work with the finer gauges of yarn. From this he recruited most of his workers, and machinery was brought from America. The company specialized in making stockings wholly or mainly of pure silk. Cotton, and at one time wool, was used for reinforcement and the 'silk' stockings of the 1920s often had cotton tops which extended well below the knee.

At first, silk was dyed and finished prior to being knitted, and the making of such fine-gauge stockings was new to everybody, including the knitters. However, in the mid-1920s the company started using raw gum silk which was easier to handle and could be dyed and finished afterwards.

In 1924, the company registered the name 'Aristoc'. It came about after A E Allen was introduced to a man who had no connection with the hosiery trade but who, on discovering that Allen was a stocking manufacturer, said: 'I've often thought that if I was a stocking manufacturer I'd call my products "Aristoc"'. With that the man said goodbye and Allen never saw nor heard of him again. An application to register 'Aristoc' was made that afternoon, although it

was two years before the name was used.

A E Allen spent a lot of time writing the word Aristoc in different ways.

Many of the big stores sold only 'own-name' brands – some were actually made at Langley Mill – and it was difficult to get them to take Aristoc. The company became Aristoc Ltd in 1934 and later W L Arber Ltd became a subsidiary. For several years it operated a three-shift system which covered twenty hours each day.

After the Second World War, nylon became available to the hosiery industry. The first British 'nylons' appeared in 1947, but the Government quickly let it be known that supplies of raw materials would be directly linked to export performance. As a result, Aristoc contributed millions of pounds to the country's foreign exchange. In 1955, Aristoc Ltd opened a factory in Ramsey in the Isle of Man.

In 1993 the company moved its manufacturing to a state-of-the-art factory in Belper, Derbyshire, where electronically controlled knitting machines, using nylon and elastane yarns, produce tights, stockings and hold-ups.

The industry has come a long way from those 39-gauge stockings produced in America in the early years of the century to the fine 7-denier stockings and tights of today. Aristoc was relaunched in 1995 with an increased market share and wider international distribution. Its current logo is very close to the original script devised by A E Allen in 1924.

Armitage Shanks marks the coming together of two long-established companies, one named after a place, the other after a person.

Appropriately, our story can be traced back to the Battle of Waterloo. In 1817, a group of North Staffordshire potters had moved to the village of Armitage, in Staffordshire, where Thomas Bond, a brickmaker, built a bottle neck kiln. Their aim was to make general earthenware (coarse pottery), but the firm went bankrupt. The pottery, however, survived.

The company was acquired by Salt and Swan in 1851. It started to make sanitary-ware, alongside the earthenware, and these are the beginnings of the present firm. The constituents of those early pieces of sani-tary-ware – ball clay from Dorset or Devon, china clay from Devon and Cornwall, flint from Kent, and sand from Cheshire – were transported by ship, canal barge or horse and cart.

As interest grew in hygiene and public health, a Public Health Act was passed in 1848 which stated that all new houses should have 'sufficient water closet or privy

FACING PAGE:
Advertisement in Vogue,
c. *1960*

ABOVE: *John Shanks*
LEFT: *Aerial view, Armitage
site, 1926*

or ashpit'; failure to comply meant a fine of £20, a lot of money in those days. Similarly, factories had to provide sufficient WCs for employees of each sex.

Although early designs were very basic, the introduction of water closets led to a reduction in the spread of disease. Britain was a pioneer in such matters and Armitage sanitary-ware was exhibited at the Great Paris Exhibition of 1855.

In 1867, the company was sold at a local auction to the Reverend Edward Johns, himself an auctioneer and Congregational minister. He afterwards said, 'If my men make sacrifices and do their best to help me, then we will pull through and our ware will be known all over the world.' As early as 1876, there was a display of Armitage ware at the Philadelphia Exhibition in America, where the famous Dolphin suite won a Golden Award.

Edward Johns's son, Edward Lewis Johns, took over the firm in 1893, but in 1900 sold it to two brothers, Alfred Henry and Edward Richard Corn, with the agreement that they would trade as Edward Johns, and this name was kept until 1960.

In the early 1900s, WCs and wash-basins were very flamboyant with elaborate gold banding and painted motifs on the basins. Some WCs were moulded into intricate designs, taking the form of animals, fish or flowers, many needing up to sixteen moulds to complete the shape. Although they gave a sense of luxury and wealth they were often unhealthy, harbouring bacteria and dirt in the crevices.

After the First World War, there was an increase in demand. In 1923, the company developed their own laboratories and two

ABOVE: *Revd Edward Johns*
LEFT: *Water closets featured in 1890 Edward Johns catalogue*
FACING PAGE, TOP: *Water closets featured in 1895 Shanks catalogue*
FACING PAGE, BELOW: *Lavatory basins featured in 1890 Edward Johns catalogue*

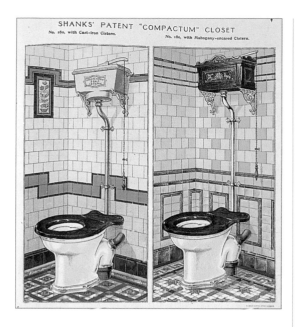

SHANKS' PATENT "COMPACTUM" CLOSET
No. 180, with Cast-iron Cistern.
No. 180, with Mahogany-encased Cistern.

foundry called the 'Tubal' foundry, based on an old Biblical name. Unfortunately, through an agreement he made with another company, he was forced out of business and became bankrupt, but the enterprise was taken over by his brother who was able to get credit. When John had paid off his creditors, the two brothers and William Shanks, Andrew's son, formed a partnership.

John Shanks had great courage and strength of character, a keen sense of humour and a determination to succeed. He was regarded as a pioneer in the sanitary business, even including systems for ships. John's son, also John, became a partner when he was twenty-one and was the first person to design a fireclay urinal stall. He took out a patent on the design but, as Shanks, at that time, made no pottery, it was taken up by Twyfords who made a great

years later they introduced pastel-coloured glazed sanitary-ware. This required new skills, for colour matching was imperative, any slight variation being easily noticed once the items were installed.

Many changes have taken place, smoother lines have been introduced and cisterns, now with levers rather than chains, have come lower down the wall. In 1930, Edward Jones & Co supplied sanitary-ware for the liner *Queen Mary*, and today its products are found in Buckingham Palace.

John Shanks was born in Paisley, Scotland, in 1826, and became a plumber. By the time he was twenty-five he was a plumber and gas fitter on his own account. He later moved to Barrhead where he was joined by his brother Andrew Ferrier Shanks.

John was an innovative young man and in 1860 he created a brass foundry on the upper floor of his plumber's shop, with the idea of manufacturing water closets. His first patent, taken out in 1864, was for a closet with a plunger valve, and with a ball-cock. Following the success of this he built a brass

NEW PORCELAINE ROYALE (NON CRAZING)
LAVATORIES WITH PATENT RECESSED FRONT.
Patent No. 18,944.

No. J 201—Decorated "New Tiger Lily."

No. J 201—Decorated "Chrysanthemum" Pattern.

No. J 201—Decorated "Azalia" and Marble.

SANITARY EARTHENWARE

success of it. After John Jnr had visited America, Shanks introduced a marble-top lavatory with nickel plate brass legs, similar to one he had seen there; it sold all over the world.

About 1900, the company opened a showroom at 81 New Bond Street to enable it to obtain a larger share of the West End trade. Just before this, it built its own pottery to produce sanitary fireclay. In 1901, it exhibited in the Palace of Industry at the International Exhibition in Glasgow and, for a fee of £1,000, won a concession to install all the sanitary fixtures in the conveniences throughout the Exhibition. The company was allowed to keep all the pennies (old) placed in the slots for the use of the WCs and the twopences for the use of the wash-basin or cloak-room. At the end of the six-month Exhibition the takings adequately met the costs involved.

In 1897, the Metropolitan Board of Works in Melbourne, Australia, placed an order for 8,000 cisterns to be used throughout the city, and in 1909 15,000 cisterns were shipped to Argentina, followed in 1910 by an order for a further 22,000; there were also considerable markets in India, Egypt, Denmark and many British Colonies. The company also fitted out the Atlantic liner *Mauretania* with sanitary-ware and some years later installed Shanks sanitary equipment throughout the *Queen Elizabeth*.

In 1969, Armitage Ware and Shanks Holding Ltd merged and formed the Armitage Shanks Group Ltd. The following year the group established a factory in Iran to enable them to supply outlets and special commissions in the Middle East.

Today Armitage Shanks manufacture and supply baths and wash-basins moulded in plastic, as well as items made of fireclay. Edward Johns was indeed prophetic when he said that 'our ware will be known all over the world' for its orders have included installations at the Merlin Hotel in Kuala Lumpur, the Royal Hilton Hotel in Tehran, and the Ashoka Hotel in New Delhi. In Britain, even the Prime Minister uses its facilities – Armitage Shanks sanitary fittings are installed in 10 Downing Street.

LEFT: *Armitage Shanks 1997 Liberty suite*

FACING PAGE, LEFT: *'It doesn't affect the heart' was often stated in advertisements*
FACING PAGE, RIGHT: *Window display in early 1940s*

ASPRO

At the outbreak of the First World War, the German chemical group Bayer held the patent for Aspirin in many countries but had not applied for one for Australia.

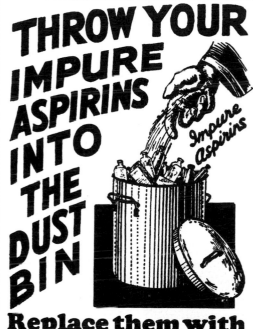

Aspirin is made from salicylic acid and acetic anhydride; the materials are heated together and pungent vapours are given off before crystals form.

George Richard Rich Nicholas, a thirty-one-year-old pharmaceutical chemist, lived in Melbourne, Australia in 1915. He was experimenting in an attempt to make the drug because supplies were not available in Australia, due to the war. He requisitioned his wife's paraffin tins, and other makeshift apparatus, but he needed a reflux condenser, a water-cooled tube, that would condense the vapours and return them as liquid to the mixture. Without one, the appalling smells filled the little pharmacy and the fumes made him ill, causing him to lose weight and temporarily lose his sight. Progress was slow. In time, he produced

aspirin of a sort – white flakes joined together in the tube, but the aspirin was impure and purification proved difficult.

One day Harry Woolf Shmith, an industrial experimenter and inventor, came to the pharmacy and offered to help George, who gladly accepted. Now the work gathered speed, but their aspirin tasted of vinegar, was brownish-pink in colour, and had a vile smell; not really a commercial proposition. Success came on 12 June 1915 and the two experimenters rushed to apply for the right to take over the Bayer trade name Aspirin; on 17 September 1915 a licence was granted. Their sample was purer than those from Bayer. The public were recommended to stop purchasing the German drug.

They still had to put the aspirin into tablet form. To do this George Nicholas's brother Alfred, his business partner J W Broady and Harry Shmith's father joined them. As losses accumulated, Broady and the Shmiths sold out their interest to the Nicholas brothers, something they later bitterly regretted.

Alfred Nicholas was a frail man with a minor malformation of his foot and an under-developed lung. He dreamed of riches.

The Nicholas brothers were greatly helped by Charles Langdon, whose company supplied the raw materials and exceptional credit facilities. Next they got a wind-the-handle tableting machine, but, although they now had production, the company's debts still grew. Gradually, the young firm increased, but there were those in government who smeared the brothers' integrity.

George and Alfred thought up and registered the odd little trade name 'Aspro'. No one is certain how it arose, although a boardroom minute from 1951 records that it is thought to be the 'AS' taken from 'NicholAS' and 'PRO' from 'PROducts'. Aspro was registered in April 1917 in Australia and shortly afterwards in other countries; it became one of the best-known names in medicine throughout the world. The government tried to destroy the company by cancelling the right to use the name Aspirin, but they had a branded product, Aspro, to offer to the public.

The product may have been secure but the company was not – it was near to bankruptcy. Fortunately, one wet December night, George Davies, a salesman representing a printing company, entered their office.

KEEP "In the Pink" THESE GREY NOVEMBER DAYS

'ASPRO' SMASHES COLDS & FLU IT'S *Got* SOMETHING

Davies brought optimism to the gloomy scene; he joined the team – at £4 a week plus 1 per cent of sales – and turned the business round. Although George Nicholas had started the company, it was Alfred who took the leading role. Alfred, a strict Methodist, when anxious about its financial state would pray about it, but he also mortgaged his furniture and risked thousands of pounds hoping that Aspro would succeed.

Davies, a failed entrepreneur, suggested that the Nicholas brothers should give away £2,000 worth of Aspro in 3d. packets, trial it in Queensland and support the plan with hard-sell advertising. More money had to be borrowed to fund the trial, but it was an outstanding success. Broadsheets were distributed throughout the area, and anyone taking a coupon to the chemist got a free packet of Aspro. The campaign then moved to Victoria with the same success; Aspro was becoming widely known and trusted. It really did cure headaches and pains, brought temperatures down and made flu-ish colds more bearable, and the public responded by coming back to

buy more. Davies also claimed it cured nervous disorders, rheumatism, sciatica, neuritis, anxiety, upset stomach, insomnia and many other problems.

In 1919, there was an influenza epidemic in Australia. To check profiteering on drugs, the government fixed the price of 'necessary commodities' and Aspro was the only proprietary brand named. Davies was delighted. He had proclaimed Aspro was a necessary commodity; now the government said so! He was establishing that Aspro was a reliable, pure, safe, predictable and effective drug.

About 1920, a member of the team went to the United States to find a new tablet-making machine and whilst there bought Sanitape, a packaging process used in the seed industry. With it tablets could be

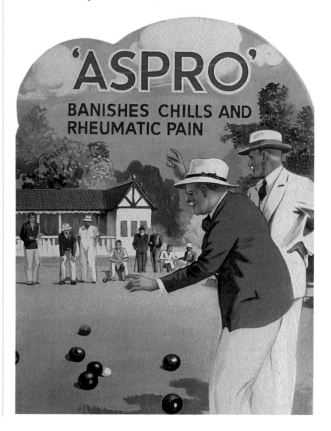

'ASPRO' BANISHES CHILLS AND RHEUMATIC PAIN

mechanically spaced on a paper tape and enclosed. Then the tape was folded into a zig-zag and waxed; the tablets were in hygienic, airtight and moisture-proof compartments. Aspro negotiated exclusive use of the process.

With all their success, Alfred was neither well nor at peace. He strove towards further expansion. Developments came in New Zealand and then in Britain where George Garcia, a Spanish Australian Jew, headed the initiative. Lancashire and Yorkshire were the launch territories, and headquarters were set up in Manchester. At first, sales were disastrous and many suggested that Aspro should cut its losses and go home, but the Nicholas brothers decided to fight on. The new strategy was to identify one town and give it the full Davies treatment. Hull was chosen, and the campaign was a complete success; a few months later Leeds was targeted with similar results. Again, an influenza epidemic came to their aid and Aspro became successful across Britain. The first British-made tablets were produced in Slough in 1927 and distribution was through grocers, sweet shops and tobacconists.

Later, Aspro appeared in Denmark, Germany, Fiji, Argentina, Egypt, and Singapore.

Differences were developing between George and Alfred Nicholas. A serious argument brought on a minor coronary thrombosis, and later a heart attack, for Alfred, and he died in 1937, aged fifty-five.

Alfred's son Maurice joined the company and George became governing director, but there was boardroom conflict as the older men took a conservative view of the company's future, whilst Maurice wanted to diversify.

After the Second World War, profits declined, but work had been done on developing agricultural and veterinary products, and continued in the Ethical Division on items for humans. It was in the mid-1950s that the famous 'Are you one degree under?' campaign was launched, and the company took on products such as Lifeguard, Radox, Rennies, Dip and Dispel. The man who had started it all, George Nicholas, died in 1960, aged seventy-six.

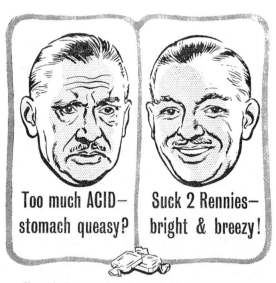

Too much ACID— stomach queasy?

Suck 2 Rennies— bright & breezy!

You can't digest your food if your stomach glands don't release enough acid . . . but they sometimes overdo it, giving you acid indigestion. Trying to relieve that with heavy antacid doses can overdo it the other way, arresting the pain but leaving too little acid for digestion to go on, which brings on even worse pain later. The way to neutralize the acid just enough to end the pain is with Rennies which, as you suck them slowly like sweets, trickle antacid juices in, drip by drip. Just the help that Nature needed! If that does not help you, do see your doctor.

DIGESTIF **RENNIES**   Separately wrapped— for purse or pocket

BALLY

The Bally family had produced ribbons in the monastic village of Schoenenwerd, in Switzerland, since the end of the eighteenth century. In the 1840s, Carl Franz Bally, who was born in 1821, took over the part of the family business that specialized in elastic ribbon production, a new product at that time.

In 1850, Carl went on a business trip to Paris and, for the first time in his life, he paid a visit to a shoe manufacturer. It made a lasting impression on him, not least because the fashion in shoes at that time dictated an elastic insert, something he felt could easily be made from Bally elastic ribbon.

In 1851, he began producing shoes in Schoenenwerd, a difficult undertaking in those early days when all his shoes would be made by hand, but gradually machinery was introduced. A few years later, European immigrants living in South America sought European shoes and to meet that demand Bally began exporting there in 1857.

The innovative strength of Bally was immense; Carl regularly made visits to England and the United States to inspect the latest production methods and to bring himself up to date with the latest fashion in shoes.

As shoe production expanded, retail stores were also developed; the first was opened in Geneva in 1865, but others quickly followed in Montevideo, Buenos Aires, Paris and London. Carl Franz Bally died in 1899.

There are now Bally factories in Switzerland, France and England, and Bally is still known worldwide for the quality of its shoes and for the part it plays in creating shoes which lead the way in fashion and style.

'Marquise' a new high fronted satin pump by Bally of Switzerland

Bally

IN LONDON AT
116 NEW BOND ST.   30 OLD BOND ST
260 REGENT ST. 22 SLOANE ST.
132 KING'S RD. 49 GOLDERS GREEN RD
ALSO MANCHESTER AND BRISTOL

"Bally"

SCHUHE
IMPORTE DE SUISSE

FACING PAGE, TOP: *Advertisement from 1941*
FACING PAGE, BELOW: *Advertisement from 1952*

ABOVE: *Advertisement in* Vogue, *1965*
LEFT: *Late 1920s' advertisement*

John Polson was born in Caithness in the latter part of the eighteenth century, but some years later moved to Paisley. In earlier days, the Caithness area had been the centre of the kelp industry – the gathering of seaweed – but in Paisley John became a weaver. He had two sons, John jnr and William, who built up a thriving muslin manufacturing business in the town.

In the early nineteenth century another firm, William Brown & Son, moved their muslin manufacturing business from Glasgow to Paisley, the centre of a developing textile industry. Where there are textile mills there is a need for starch production. Brown, Johnstone & Co, part of Brown & Son's muslin business, produced buckram which needed large

amounts of starch for stiffening. Both companies needed better facilities and, in 1840, John Polson jnr and Brown's formed a partnership to set up a bleaching, scouring and starching works – Brown & Polson had been formed. Their first product was a 'Powder

Starch' made from sago flour, which was put on the market in 1842, and it received a Certificate of Merit at the Great Exhibition of 1851.

John, however, began to use maize, or Indian corn, as his source of starch, registering a patent for the process in 1854. It was accepted that western stomachs did not readily digest corn and, although it was used for cattle food, it was not used by millers as a source of flour, even in time of famine. Through the processes John used

Corn Flour prepared with milk is wholesome every-day fare for the children.

Children are so well nourished and warmed with such dishes as corn flour soup, baked pudding, and hot custard that it should form a daily part of their diet.

Use good sweet milk, and when buying Corn Flour choose Brown and Polson's "Patent"—the finest example of Corn Flour manufactured.

Use only the small quantities of this Corn Flour noted in the recipes, because it goes so far. Cook thoroughly, boiling 10 minutes. All stewed fruits—apples, prunes, figs, etc.— go splendidly with corn flour puddings.

Brown and Polson's "Patent" Corn Flour

An all round food for all the year round

he discovered that a finely ground corn starch was readily digested, and in the same year he produced 'Brown & Polson's Patent Corn Flour'. Colman's had used the term

'corn flour' previously for a rice starch, known as 'Colman's Corn-Flour'. It took on a new meaning as Brown & Polson's edible corn starch became the basis for blancmanges, custards, baby and invalid foods, and a thickener for soups and gravies, as contained in Mrs Beeton's recipes! The name lost its capital letter and became known as 'cornflour'.

John Polson jnr, the inventor of cornflour, died in 1900, aged seventy-five. By then he was a millionaire and one of the richest industrialists in the west of Scotland.

The company moved site as growing prosperity demanded, finally settling at the Carriagehill Works, in Paisley. As the company expanded, its advertising grew, not on house walls, but on railway stations and, from 1860, in many of Britain's newspapers. From quite early days it also produced a series of cookery books advocating the use of cornflour.

FACING PAGE, LEFT: *John Polson jnr (top), John Brown (below)*
FACING PAGE, BELOW RIGHT: *Paisley factory,* Illustrated News, *1860*
FACING PAGE, TOP RIGHT, AND THIS PAGE, TOP: *Illustrations from a 1930s' recipe booklet*
LEFT: *1909 advertisement in* Christian Herald
RIGHT: *Early packaging*

BY APPOINTMENT
TO HIS MAJESTY KING GEORGE V

BROWN & POLSON'S

PATENT CORN FLOUR

THE BEST QUALITY.

GUARANTEED PERFECTLY PURE.

Recommended for Children's and Invalids' Diet with Milk, for BLANC-MANGE, CUSTARDS, PUDDINGS, &c., AND SUITABLE FOR

THICKENING SOUPS, SAUCES, &C.

BROWN & POLSON, LTD., PAISLEY & LONDON.

Following the death of John Polson jnr, the business was continued by J Armour Brown and his three sons, later joined by Lord Rowallan who was connected by marriage to the Polson family. In 1881, in a 'Treatise on the manufacture of Starch, etc.' by Robert Hutter of Philadelphia, it was described as 'among the most gigantic establishments of the kind'.

By 1930, Brown & Polson Ltd had become the sole producer of dry starches from wet-milling, but its plant was old and required large injections of new capital. In 1935, Brown & Polson Ltd became a wholly-owned subsidiary of Corn Products Company Ltd, an affiliate company of the American Corn Products Refining Company, with a manufacturing site in Manchester. In 1950, Corn Products Company Ltd changed its name to Brown & Polson Ltd, a much better known name. At this time expansion of the Manchester site took place and the Royal Starch Works at Paisley was enlarged, but, in 1964, all starch production was transferred to Manchester. In 1971 Brown & Polson Ltd once again changed its name, this time to CPC (United Kingdom) Ltd, and it is known by this company name to this day.

Over the last thirty years, CPC (United Kingdom) Ltd has sold products under many more household brands including Knorr soups and sauces, Frank Cooper's marmalade, Hellmann's

mayonnaise, Ambrosia desserts, Pot Noodle instant hot snacks, Napolina tomatoes and pasta, Bovril drink, Marmite yeast extract, Mazola corn oil and Dextro Energy glucose tablets.

The safety match was invented by Professor Gustav Erik Pasch of Sweden. He was granted a patent in 1844 and production began that year. However, they were not a success and were discontinued in 1845. In 1852, Johan Lundstrom adapted a formula which included chlorate of potash in the match-head composition, whilst amorphous phosphorus was added to a friction panel which was placed on the rubbing surface of the box, which had been sent to him by Arthur Albright of Birmingham.

William Bryant was born in 1804, the son of a starch maker from Tiverton, Devon.

The family were Wesleyan Methodists, but, in 1832, William joined the Society of Friends, marrying Ann Jago Carkeet, also a Quaker, the same year. In 1835, he and an Edward James became partners in a firm of general merchants and later also established a soap factory.

BELOW: *Bryant & May match factory at Bow in the 1860s*

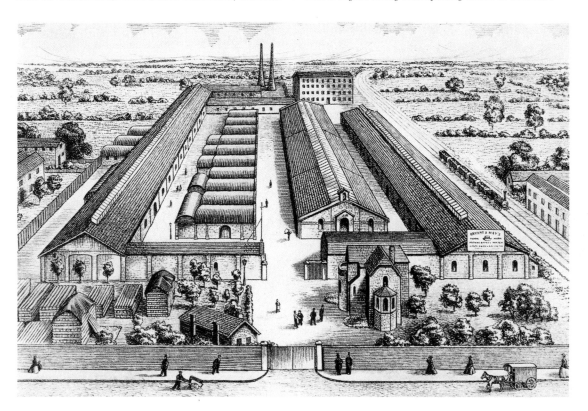

Francis May was born in 1803, the son of a prosperous merchant and Quaker. In 1822, he began a three-year apprenticeship with a grocer in Epping and later became a tea dealer and grocer in London.

In 1843, Bryant and May formed a partnership and established Bryant & May, provision merchants, at 133–4 Tooley Street and 5 Philpot Lane, London.

In 1850, Carl Lundstrom, brother of Johan, visited England to introduce the matches which they made at their factory at Jonkoping, Sweden. He visited all the major match importers but, when he could not make satisfactory arrangements to trade, the customs office suggested he went to see Bryant & May.

Later Lundstrom wrote that Francis May was 'an elderly gentleman, and judging from his clothing a Quaker'. We are told that

TOP LEFT: *The 1890s' Family Match Safe, containing thirty-six boxes of matches and three ornamental match-box cases*
ABOVE, AND FACING PAGE, TOP RIGHT: *Contemporary events and interests exploited for sales promotions*
LEFT: *Production unit at Fairfield Works in the 1870s*
FACING PAGE, LEFT: *Lion label, c. 1900*
FACING PAGE, BELOW RIGHT: *After 1959, the swan changed course and swam towards the right*

his face beamed with kindness and benevolence, while Bryant is described as a 'rather stiff man of dignified appearance'. They inspected Lundstrom's matches and gave him an initial order. Gradually the orders grew until they were never for less

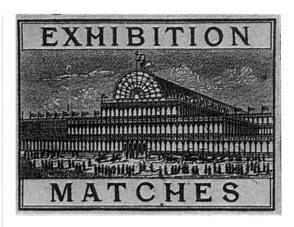

than fifty cases at one time, and not infrequently the order was for up to 500 cases, each case holding fifty gross of boxes: 720,000 matches! In exchange Bryant & May sold the Lundstroms large quantities of uncut wax taper for them to manufacture vestas, matches made with waxed taper rather than wood.

Soon the Swedish company could not meet the demand and Bryant & May built its own factory in London, the Lundstroms selling it the British Patent Rights in 1855 for £100. Match production began at the Fairfield Works at Bow in 1861 and soon the firm was making several million matches each week.

Before that time, match making was mainly a cottage industry, but Bryant & May developed modern production methods. The splints, however, were machine-cut to the length of two matches. Girls then placed the splints in a machine which arranged them in 'dipping-frames'. The frames were dipped in paraffin to increase the flammability of the splints before both ends were dipped in an igniting composition. The splints were then hand cut into two matches before the exact number was counted by hand into each box!

At one time, Bryant & May had five factories in the United Kingdom and numerous interests in overseas companies, but in 1994, the company stopped manufacturing and now sources all its matches from its sister companies. In 1997, the company became Swedish Match UK Ltd.

BUTTERICK

For countless generations women have made clothes for their family, but it has not always been as easy as it is today. The tape measure was not invented until the 1820s, and it was about 1840 that the sewing machine and the paper pattern were conceived.

Ebenezer Butterick was born in Massachusetts in the United States, the seventh child of Ruhamah and Francis Butterick. When he left school he worked in his brother's village store where he learned a lot about business, but he did not like shop work. He left the store to become an apprentice tailor, found that he quickly acquired the new skills, and eventually became a merchant tailor in Fitchburg.

In 1850, Ebenezer married his childhood sweetheart, Ellen Pollard. The couple had two children and, as he worked at his tailoring, he watched his wife making clothes for the children. He felt there must be easier ways to ensure the clothes fitted correctly and he started experimenting. He cut stiff paper into shapes, then snipped the fabric round them and sewed up the pieces. In 1863, he cut out his first complete, perfect pattern on the living-room table. This pattern was for a shirt for his four-year-old nephew, Clarence Butterick.

At that time Garibaldi was a great hero and Butterick scaled down some of the distinctive outfits he wore, for small boys; he also made replicas for children of zouave braided jackets which were worn in the American Civil War. Soon he told his wife, with great enthusiasm, that pattern-making was to be his new business.

All the members of both his and his wife's families were called in to help fold the first patterns. They were boxed in hundreds and sold to retailers at $10 a box; Ebenezer kept the first $10 bill he received as a happy souvenir.

Within a few months, demand for the patterns exceeded his ability to supply and extra rooms had to be rented in the neighbourhood. Half a dozen women and girls were soon employed, folding and packing the patterns.

As the business grew, he also involved Abner Pollard, his brother-in-law, as his secretary, and Jones Wilder as his selling agent – it was Jones Wilder who pointed out that there would be an even greater demand for patterns for women's clothes, which proved to be the case.

A New York Office was opened and the three men became directors of the newly formed 'E Butterick & Company'. The factory operations were also transferred to New York and, in 1873, the company introduced *The Metropolitan*, its

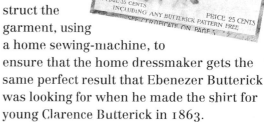

own fashion magazine, which later became known as *The Delineator*. Fashions at that time included many tucks and frills and these garments took a lot of patience to make, but for some it was a time of leisure and, through interest in such magazines, women developed a great interest in fashion.

In 1871, Butterick's sold six million patterns and by 1876 had opened branches in London, Paris and Vienna. In 1881, the Butterick Publishing Company Limited was formed, with Jones Wilder as president. Ebenezer Butterick became its secretary. He had been aware for a long time that his interest was not primarily in making money, but in the creative side of the business. Gradually, he withdrew from commerce to devote more time and some of his fortune to the welfare of poor children.

In 1904, a new sixteen-storey building was opened in New York; on its wall was the name Butterick in letters sixty feet high. Every working day of the year forty-five tons of paper were used as the demand for patterns grew. New magazines soon appeared, including the *Butterick Quarterly*, for which Maude Humphreys Bogart, the mother of Humphrey Bogart, was an artist.

Each year, Butterick manufactures several million patterns, to be used by women in many countries of the world. Initially, a basic paper pattern is made and the details are transferred on to a muslin pattern which is then cut out. From the muslin pattern a heavy paper pattern is traced, which becomes the 'Master Pattern Block'. One of Butterick's own dressmakers will then construct the garment, using a home sewing-machine, to ensure that the home dressmaker gets the same perfect result that Ebenezer Butterick was looking for when he made the shirt for young Clarence Butterick in 1863.

FACING PAGE, TOP LEFT: *Ebenezer Butterick*
FACING PAGE, TOP RIGHT: *Butterick follows the Paris line with black day-dresses in 1938*
FACING PAGE, BELOW: *The popular 'silk tub frock' of Summer 1925*
THIS PAGE: *Front covers of catalogues*

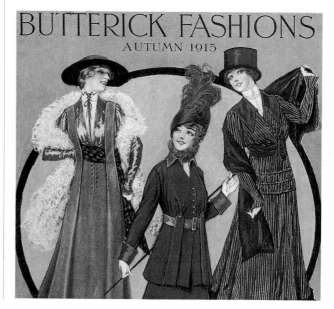

The first liquefied petroleum (LP) gas was probably produced by the Riverside Oil Company in Britain, but there was concern at the risk of gas escaping and its potentials were unknown.

In the United States, the American Gasoil Co was formed and started using gas on a commercial scale; in 1911 it was used to cut steel. The first domestic LP gas installation took place in 1912 in Waterford, Pennsylvania and, in 1920, after much experimentation, the Carbide and Carbon Chemicals Corporation marketed 'Pyrofax'. LP gas was here to stay.

A contract to import French butane into England was agreed in December 1934, but capital was needed to develop its uses and introduce it to the British market. Ritchie Gill, a Cornishman, had worked in the United States and had seen butane gas in use. Gill had little money to invest, but was intro-duced to Captain C R E Jorgensen, a London stock-broker, who raised the necessary funds. A company was formed to market the new bottled gas, for which Ritchie had coined the name 'Calor Gas', this being derived from 'calorie', a unit of heat energy.

The Modern Gas & Equipment Company Ltd was incorporated in 1935 with a nomial capital of £3, in £1 shares. The monies needed to start the company were £700, provided by Ritchie, and a £3,000 loan, arranged by Captain Jorgensen. Its first premises were a rented office in Margaret Street, London.

At this time, the British oil refining industry was small, but fifty full butane cylinders and a few appliances were imported from France. The Customs officers regarded them as a dangerous consignment and other sources were sought. Shell Mex and BP Ltd made supplies available from the Anglo Iranian Company's refinery at Llandarcy in South Wales, although previously they

ABOVE: *Advertisement in* The Countryman, *1939*
LEFT: *Early mobile display caravan*
FACING PAGE, TOP: The Gas Times *magazine cover 1935*
FACING PAGE, BELOW: *Calor Gas sponsors the 1948 Olympic Games*

had not thought the separation of butane was worthwhile.

No LP gas cylinders had ever been made in Britain – the Home Office rejected the French specifications – and new specifications were drawn up by the chief metallurgist of Imperial Chemical Industries and the Home Office, which were used by Joseph Sankey & Sons of Bilston in the West Midlands. ICI were producing petrol from coal at their Billingham chemical complex by means of a hydrogenation process, and liquefied petroleum was produced as a by-product.

It was realized that rural communities, as well as municipally owned and private gas companies, would be important markets for the new product and, to provide extra capital, a private limited company was formed. The *Gas Times*, on 20 July 1935, published a five-page article on 'Calor Gas', commending it to gas undertakings as a way of increasing business.

The Calor Gas (Distributing) Co Ltd was formed in August 1935 with a capital of £25,000. Captain Jorgensen became chairman and Ritchie Gill general manager, Ritchie choosing to draw no salary but to receive a fixed sum for every ton of butane sold, a potentially bigger remuneration for a keen salesman.

The initiative bore fruit and the *Calor Gas News* of January 1936 had a guaranteed circulation of 100,000 copies. It illustrated the many uses for the new fuel – lighting a church near Canterbury, lighting a cow-house near Broadway, and also the lighting and the heating of a hot-plate in a caravan. Over succeeding years, LP gas has

become accepted as the universal energy supply in caravans; it was also used for lighting temporary road signs in remote locations.

In 1936, major marketing initiatives took place and it was decided not only to employ salesmen but also to appoint firms as dealers, responsible for installations and deliveries of LP gas. Decentralization took place and, in each area, salesmen were provided with a small Ford 8hp van, painted in cream with red lettering. The van was fitted up inside as a miniature showroom, with a gas cylinder connected to a cooker, gas-ring, a two-burner hot-plate, and a small fire. Cookery demonstrations were organized at Women's Institute meetings, and also in conjunction with Cadbury's; the Calor Gas salesman, and his van, would be there with a ready supply of literature.

Over the years, the number of installations has grown enormously, especially in rural areas. LP gas is also used extensively in leisure interests, particularly for caravans and barbecue stoves; in industry it supplies heat for blower heaters, and for oxy-propane burners for cutting steel. LP gas is now being more widely used in commercial vehicles because of its clean exhausts. New benefits are constantly being discovered for this versatile fuel.

John Cash was born in 1822, his brother Joseph in 1826 – they were the eldest sons of Joseph Cash of Sherbourne House in Coventry. Their father was a Quaker stuff merchant and a leading businessman in the city. After serving seven-year apprenticeships with stuff merchants, the brothers operated a ribbon business which used outworkers, but, in 1846, they built a steam-

a clear case for Cash's WOVEN NAME TAPES

powered factory which they equipped with Jacquard looms. They recruited French designers to design their silk ribbons, which were popular for sewing on the gowns of the fashion-conscious Victorian ladies, and, by 1856, Cash's had 200 weavers in the factory. They paid some of the highest wages in the ribbon industry until 1857, when they were forced to pay lower wage rates imposed by Coventry masters.

Partly influenced by their Quaker principles, and also wishing to retain in part the outworker system, the brothers planned to build 100 'top shops', or cottage factories, arranged around a square, where the attic-level looms were powered by a central beam engine. Unfortunately, the trade boom did not last long and only forty-eight terraced houses were built at the site outside the city centre. However, Cash's did encourage the formation of a dramatic society, sports clubs and evening classes.

The Anglo-French Trade Treaty of 1860 brought an influx of low-priced French ribbons, but, although many firms collapsed, J & J Cash survived. It took out a patent in 1860 for the manufacture of narrow frillings, but the hard economic climate meant that it had to exercise a much tougher line with staff than previously. However, the brothers were philanthropic towards the city, making numerous gifts to

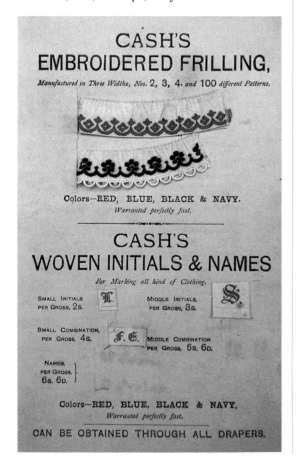

local charities; John also served as a Liberal on Coventry City Council from 1868 to 1876.

Both brothers died in 1880, the partnership being taken over by John's son, Sidney, and his cousin Joseph. About this time, the company started weaving labels for manufacturers to identify their own products, and also made woven name tapes for sewing on to household linen and items of clothing. This became an excellent line for the company, particularly when larger numbers of children attended boarding schools. In 1964, J & J Cash

was appointed 'Manufacturers of Woven Name Tapes to Her Majesty the Queen' and was awarded a Royal Warrant to HRH The Prince of Wales for this line in January 1997. However, as fewer children wear school uniform, they have wisely diversified into making a range of related products. Now the sole survivor of those historic Coventry weavers, and using computerized technology, the company produces attractive small woven pictures, braces, badges, and silk gifts which make ideal presents and have become collectors' items. Its products are marketed in Western Europe, North America, and the Far East.

FACING PAGE, TOP: *Advertisement in* Homes and Gardens
FACING PAGE, BELOW: *Very early showcard*
ABOVE: *Advertisement in* Women's Journal, *1953*
LEFT AND BELOW: *Modern woven bookmark and greetings card*

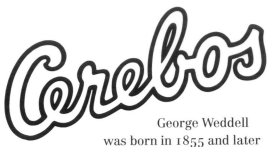

George Weddell was born in 1855 and later became a chemist with Mawson, Swan and Weddell in Newcastle upon Tyne. As his daughter was a poorly child, George decided to add something to her diet to strengthen her bones and teeth. Although vitamins and trace elements were unheard of at this time, he mixed small quantities of magnesium carbonate and calcium phosphate with the family's household salt. He was so pleased with the result that he felt it would be good to supply this 'enriched' salt to the general public.

At the salt works at Greatham, in County Durham, rock salt existed in a large bed about 1,000 feet below the surface. By adding water to the bed, this salt was converted into brine, which was then pumped to the surface and processed, using the old 'open pan' method.

In a building in Picton Terrace, Newcastle, alongside the River Tyne, the ground floor was occupied by a firm of boot and shoe manufacturers, whilst the upper floors were used by Cerebos Salt. Exactly how the name came about is unclear, but the following doggerel may hold some clues:

> 'Ceres' is Greek for the goddess of grain,
> 'Cerebrum' stands for the best of the brain,
> 'Bos' is an ox, and 'Os' is a bone –
> A rare combination, as critics will own.

George Weddell became chairman and managing director of Cerebos Salt and employed a manager, a chemist, an engineer and a small group of workers who did the packing. Soon, they appointed a salesman, William Collins, who later became chairman and a millionaire, and also received a knighthood. In addition to salt, the company sold baking powder and their own brand of health salts, called Seraph.

The coarse salt arrived in hundredweight sacks. It was treated and then packed into tins holding 1½lbs. Cerebos Salt was much more free-running than the old-fashioned coarse blocks, which the housewife had to crush before the salt could be put in a salt cellar. By 1896, they had salesmen covering many parts of the United Kingdom. Many of the staff were laid off in 1897 but, in the following year, were re-

LEFT: *'Blooming health'*
FACING PAGE, LEFT: *Advertisement in* Illustrated, *1948*
FACING PAGE, RIGHT: *Advertisement in* Woman, *1960*

Try these new recipes!

FREE Recipe Book Here's a wealth of exciting ideas to brighten up today's fare. Tasty dishes with a new 'twist'—all simple to prepare. Get your free copy by writing direct to Cerebos Limited, Willesden, London, N.W.10.

Ah! **BISTO**

FOR ALL MEAT DISHES

In 1898 the company moved into larger works premises in St Mary's Place and offices in Ellison Place. In 1900, George Weddell's attention was drawn to small traces of arsenic found in the phosphates they were using. This certainly caused alarm but it was found that they were very minute quantities and steps were taken to remove any impurities.

Cerebos embarked on a programme of advertising which included giving away salt cellars and spoons in return for coupons which were placed in the tins of salt. In 1904, the firm became Cerebos Ltd and also about that time introduced Saxa Salt, but unfortunately the origins of that brand have been lost. In 1906, the manufacturing process was moved to Greatham, where wells were drilled to enable the brine to be brought to the surface. Now the company had its own supplies of prime material.

It is said that Bisto was developed following discussions between the wives of two of the executives of the company. They asked their husbands to create

Ah! **LOVELY**

ah! **BISTO**

Who can resist roast pork? Crisp crunchy crackling . . . tender white meat . . . and every morsel juicy with flavour. Every mouthful made super-savoury by Bisto gravy. Ah! Bisto makes all meat dishes.

employed to make up thousands of small sample packets. These samples, about the size of a match box, were sent to doctors and chemists for their opinion and reports, and gradually the public became aware of this enriched Cerebos Salt. Young William Collins was a man of drive, even selling the salt from door to door.

"Right away!"

How exactly that describes the way Cerebos Salt pours from its hygienic container. No matter how damp the atmosphere the pure white crystals come pouring out at the first tilt. No clogging, no lumps, no waste. This is why housewives insist that it is actually a wise economy to pay the little more for Cerebos.

CEREBOS
TABLE SALT
Saves in the long run

something which could ensure a good gravy and a combination of flour, salt and colouring was the husbands' recipe. Apparently, the name comes from the first letters of the phrase 'Browns, Seasons, Thickens in one Operation', these being rearranged into BISTO.

When George Weddell died in 1916, William Collins took over as chairman. It was about this time that the famous poster appeared of a little boy pouring salt on the tail of a bird, bearing the caption 'See how it runs'. Later, Will Owen, the artist, created the poster of a boy and girl with tattered clothing inhaling the aroma from an open hot pie and exclaiming, 'Ah! Bisto.'

In 1919, the Middlewich Salt Co Ltd was acquired and the labour force grew to 850 women and 150 men. By 1931, the full effects of the Depression were being felt and, one week, without warning, each wage packet contained a note to say the recipient's contract was terminated, but anyone who wished to do so could start again on Monday morning, at the specified reduced rate of pay. Meanwhile, the dividend to shareholders rose to twenty-five per cent!

In 1942, the factory was badly damaged when eight bombs were dropped on the site.

The factory closed for VE-Day came and later the board granted all workers an extra week's pay as a special celebration.

After the war, new methods of salt production were introduced from the United States and the company also acquired other salt companies. Today, Cerebos is part of RHM Foods Group.

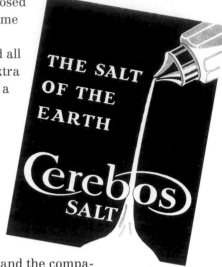

THE SALT OF THE EARTH

Cerebos SALT

LEFT: *Advertisement in* Vogue, *1953*
BELOW: *Advertisement in* Homes and Gardens, *1951*

FACING PAGE, RIGHT: *Advertisement in* Punch, *1953*

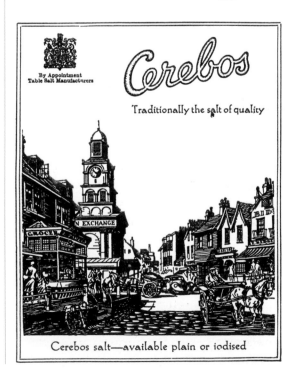

By Appointment
Table Salt Manufacturers

Cerebos

Traditionally the salt of quality

Cerebos salt—available plain or iodised

CHRISTY
HEAD·WEAR

A familiar sight in many men's outfitters are the large red hat boxes bearing the name 'Christys' London'. Behind that name is a tradition going back over two hundred years.

Miller Christy was born at Ormiston Lodge, Co Haddington, Scotland, in 1748, the fifth and youngest son of John and Mary Miller. His father was a bleacher whose family originally came from Aberdeen, had migrated to Ireland and then had settled in Ormiston, near Edinburgh. In 1763 the young lad was bound as an apprentice to his cousin and brother-in-law William Miller, Hatter Burgess of Edinburgh, to learn the 'Art and Mystery of Feltmaking'.

Miller Christy

The apprenticeship should have lasted seven years but was broken by mutual consent in 1768, and Miller Christy and Joseph Storrs set up as Storrs and Christy, hat manufacturers, at 5 White Hart Court, Gracechurch Street, in the City of London in 1773. The premises were rented from the Fishmongers' Company. Miller was quickly admitted to the Feltmakers' Company of London and served as its Master in 1792–3. The business must have prospered for in 1788 it moved to larger premises in

Gracechurch Street and, a few years later, opened a factory near Bermondsey Church, south of the Thames. In 1794, Storrs retired and the business became entirely Christy's.

The Christys were members of the Society of Friends and Miller Christy was married at the old Quaker Meeting House, about fifty yards from where his business started. The usual Friends' Declaration, or Certificate of Marriage, was signed by many well-known City Quakers and it is certain that, in the initial stages of the business, the Friends contributed largely to the success of the enterprise.

Miller Christy retired in 1804 and died in 1820. He was succeeded by his three eldest sons, Thomas, William Miller and John, and in 1826 Christys took over T & J Worsley, who were hat manufacturers at Underbank in Stockport and suppliers to Christys. In those early days dyeing came to a standstill in frosty weather, labour relations were not

were made at the company's Old Hillgate Mill in Stockport, and samples were shown at the Great Exhibition of 1851. Later, a separate company, W M Christy & Sons, was formed to concentrate on towels. Henry Christy went on to become a Fellow of the Royal Society and a recognized authority on the history of prehistoric man.

It is recorded in *The Times* that, on 27 May 1851, 'A gratifying course, with regard to their workmen and The Great Exhibition was adopted yesterday by one of our leading manufacturing firms. Messrs J T and H Christy and Co of Gracechurch Street gave a holyday (*sic*) to the whole of the persons in their employ (upward of 600), paying the cost of admission, and also of their conveyance to and from the building.'

Over succeeding years, six generations of the Christy family have played their part in maintaining the name of their founder and their reputation for hats. In 1996, control came into the hands of Maurice Pinto, the owner of Priory Investments, who, as a keen rider, had worn Christy Beaufort hats for many years. The new owners are committed to retain Christys' reputation as quality hatters.

always good and the coach service to London could be unpredictable. By 1860, the process for making hats, caps and helmets had been mechanized, and the factory site covered about twelve acres.

An announcement in the *Stockport Advertiser* on 16 December 1824 indicated that William Miller Christy, along with John Worsley (the hat manufacturer), and Isaac Lloyd and John Kenyon Winterbottom were to open a bank in Stockport. They paid 3,000 guineas for Underbank Hall. An earlier bank had failed, but these four men had such qualities that their bank soon gained the confidence of local people. It issued its own banknotes and gave the hatters financial advantage over those in other towns and Stockport became a centre for hat making. Following several mergers, the bank is now part of National Westminster Bank.

Henry Christy, a grandson of Miller Christy, visited the East and from the Sultan's palace in Constantinople he brought back the first Turkish towels seen in this country. From these examples, similar ones

Chubb

Charles Chubb was born in 1772 at Fordingbridge in Hampshire; his brother Jeremiah was born eighteen years later. They were both apprenticed to a blacksmith in Winchester and, in 1804, Charles moved to Daniel Street, Portsea, the dockland area of modern Portsmouth, where he opened a shop specializing in naval ironmongery. Unlike an ordinary ironmonger, he concentrated on the metal parts peculiar to sailing ships and also repaired specialist equipment.

In the years following the Battle of Waterloo, when people flooded to towns and cities due to the growth of industry, there was a great increase in crime. This brought a demand for stricter security, especially following a serious robbery in the Portsmouth dockyard. The crime had been committed by the use of false keys, and a government reward of £100 was offered for a lock which could only be opened by its own key. A lock designed and made by Jeremiah Chubb won the competition, and was patented in 1818 as the 'Detector

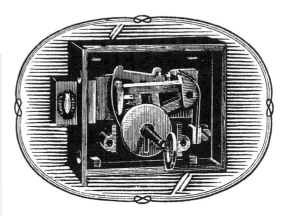

THE CHUBB
Detector Lock
Patented *in* 1818. The FORERUNNER of the *famous* CHUBB LOCKS of to-day which are now made by *grandsons* and *great-grandsons* of CHARLES CHUBB, the original Patentee

CHUBB & SONS LOCK & SAFE Co. LTD. *Bankers' Engineers and Strong Room Builders* 128 Queen Victoria Street, London, E.C.4 *Factories:* Wolverhampton

Lock' – during the firm's first half century over two and a half million of these locks were made.

Before Queen Victoria introduced her 'Royal Warrants' in 1837, Chubb had held

FACING PAGE, TOP: *1950s' advertisement*
FACING PAGE, BELOW: *The famous red hat boxes*

TOP RIGHT: *Advertisement in* Punch, *1931*
RIGHT: *Charles Chubb, 1772–1846*

CHUBB AND SONS
LOCK & SAFE Co, Ld

CHUBB'S
LOCKS
AND
SAFES

AH! THATS A
NAME I NEVER
DID LIKE

128, QUEEN VICTORIA St, E.C

a Special Licence, granted by George IV in 1823, making it one of the oldest Royal Warrant holders in the country. In 1828, customers included the Duke of Wellington, who bought four locks and a new key for Apsley House, and the Bank of England, which took two locks costing six guineas each. In 1841 Charles Chubb was appointed lockmaker to the Prince Consort.

Locksmiths had been established in the Wolverhampton area since at least the sixteenth century and Charles Chubb opened a factory there in 1830. The original works were in Temple Street, but later moved to St James's Square and then to Horseley Fields. A London shop was opened at 57 St Paul's Churchyard in 1820 and another one at 64 Old Broad Street some years later. The Portsmouth premises remained until 1835,

the same year that the company took out its first patent for a burglar-resisting safe. By now its attention was mainly given to the manufacture of safes, vaults, safe deposits, locks and associated hardware. Case-hardened steel plating was added to the interior surfaces of safes to increase protection against boring and drilling; fireproofing was improved by successive linings of sheet metal being interspersed with layers of slow heat conducting materials such as burnt brick, wood ash and coarse sand. In 1836, the first fire test of a Chubb safe took place when papers were enclosed in a Chubb patent fireproof box and exposed to the furnace of a steam engine. The box became red hot in three minutes and remained in that state for some time. When removed, the papers were completely undamaged.

Although attempts were made by competitors at home and abroad to discredit Chubb locks, the *Wolverhampton Chronicle* accorded victory to Charles Chubb: 'It is sufficient for the patentee to show that his lock is impervious under the ordinary circumstances to which locks are exposed . . . We warmly congratulate the patentee upon the conclusive triumph of an invention which confers so much honour upon his skill, and promises such vast advantages to the persons and property of the public.' By the 1840s 'Chubb' had become a household word, appearing in playbills and popular verses.

In 1847, 'Chubb's Box and Lock Mart' was opened in India by its agent, Eduljee Pestonjee. The business was carried on by his son and partner, John. John's interest in security extended beyond the care of valuables. In 1847 he wrote a letter to *The Times* on the subject of railway safety, resulting in the introduction of communication cords.

The Great Exhibition of 1851 brought the firm publicity – and a challenge. One of its

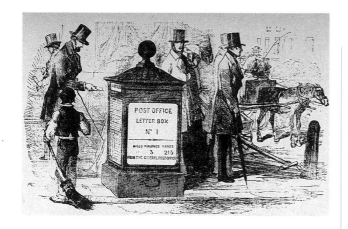

locks was successfully picked and had to be modified. (The modification prevented the insertion of two picks into a lock and foiled the lock picker.) However, Chubb was exonerated when the Superintendent of Police at the Great Exhibition stated publicly that, in twenty-seven years' experience as a police officer, he had never known a robbery be committed by picking a Chubb lock, and that the circumstances under which this had been achieved were artificial and unlike anything a burglar would encounter. Queen Victoria wrote in her journal for 10 June 1851, following a visit to the Exhibition:

Chubb locks were the 1st exhibits we regularly inspected, & they really are wonderful, of every shape and size. He [John Chubb?] explained to us the ingenious manner by which an attempt to force the lock is discovered . . .

In 1856, pillar boxes were introduced in London. They were fitted with Chubb locks, as they are throughout the country to the present day.

John Chubb died in 1872 and, ten years later, his sons formed a private limited company, Chubb & Sons Lock and Safe Company Limited.

FACING PAGE: *Advertisement from 1884*
ABOVE: *The first pillar box, 1855*
RIGHT: *Steam motor lorry,* c. *1904*

A new five-storey lock works was built in Wolverhampton during 1898 and 1899. The manufacture of safes was moved completely to Wolverhampton in 1909 when a new factory was built in Wednesfield Road.

During the Second World War, the company's head offices in Queen Victoria Street, London were destroyed. Here the company manufactured steel room doors for the Admiralty, components for heavy tanks and electrical bomb release gears.

In 1946, George Hayter Chubb, created Baron Hayter in 1928, died aged ninety-eight. He had been managing director since 1882, and was chairman until 1940! After the war, the company stopped making handmade locks, except for specialist functions, preferring to offer a high degree of security at reasonable prices. New ranges of safe were introduced, along with the first British time lock and a new combination lock.

In 1948, Chubb went public, changing its name ten years later to Chubb & Son Limited. In the years that followed, it embarked upon the transition from a lock and safe maker to a broadly based international group with companies in five continents and a much wider portfolio of activities, including electronic security, fire protection and manned guarding.

Alfred, Thomas and William were the sons of Thomas and Eliza Church, born in Northampton. Their father was a master cordwainer (shoemaker) and, on leaving school, they too became apprenticed in the shoe industry.

In 1873, the three brothers started their own business with small premises in Northampton. They would cut and stitch the leather uppers, but the lasting, making and finishing of the shoes was done by skilled hand workers in their own homes. From those earliest of days, Church's shoes were known for their quality and craftsmanship, the criteria that have stayed with the company for over a century.

As their reputation became more widely known, and demand for their shoes grew, so, in the late nineteenth century, Church & Co built a six-storey factory in Duke Street, Northampton. This was equipped with the most modern machinery and from then on all footwear was produced there.

It was a German-American salesman who started Church's export sales into Europe in 1904. He did considerable business in both men's and women's shoes in several parts of the Continent, including Germany, Switzerland and Belgium. Church's shoes came in four or five widths to a size and sizes up to 12 for men and 9 for women. Although these sizings were general practice in the high-grade shoe shops in the countries where the company was now doing business, it was unusual in the United Kingdom.

'blow hot...

swing...a hot day and a hot
weather shoe, cool, confident and
proud of its own lovely line.

...blow cold'

cavalier...a 'stepping-out' shoe, for
colder days, with a crisp line, a proud flare-
up at the instep and squared-back heel.
This is a trailer-glimpse of the shoes
that we hope will soon be
on their way to you

Church's *famous English shoes*

sizes and fittings and the store being staffed by well-trained assistants. They called the shop Babers, and it is still owned by the Church family.

Church's became a private limited company in 1926, and, in 1951, was converted to a public company. In 1929, the company opened its first store in New York's prestigious Madison Avenue. As part of a policy of having their own retail outlets, in 1954 it opened concessions in Austin Reed's stores and started to acquire retail shoe businesses. A Jones & Sons was taken over in 1955 and Joseph Cheaney & Sons Ltd in 1967. Other developments also took place to enlarge the company's international presence and it is now possible to buy Church's shoes in almost any capital city through the developed world.

From 1907, Church's men's shoes were sold into the United States and Canada, but when the First World War brought their European trade to a close, new markets were opened in South Africa, India and Argentina. After the war, the factory at Northampton was modernized and a range of women's welted shoes was introduced, with a built-in arch support. Like the men's shoes, Church's Archmoulded Shoes were available in four or five widths and they sold in large quantities.

In 1921, using private resources, members of the Church family opened a store in Oxford Street, London, where women could buy shoes which fitted correctly. This required the stocking of a large range of

FACING PAGE, TOP: *Alfred Church*
FACING PAGE, BELOW: *Thomas Owen Church*
ABOVE: *Early 1950s' advertisement*
RIGHT: *The 'vintage' Balmoral shoe*

Coats Crafts UK

At the end of the eighteenth century, George Coats, who came from a family of farmers and shepherds, moved to live on the east side of the River Cart in Paisley. He was a weaver and, in 1763, he married Catherine Heywood. They had a son James, born in 1774, who completed his apprenticeship as a weaver but then joined the cavalry, serving six years in the Ayrshire Fencibles.

In 1802, James set up in business as a weaver and later joined another weaver, James Whyte, to find a way of making Canton crêpe. The Canton crêpe shawl was a fashionable item at that time, and it is suggested that James, on one of his visits to London, had bought one for his wife. All the beautiful crêpe weaves came from China and no attempt had been made to manufacture this material in Scotland. It

was made of silk and the process required special knowledge and skill, although some silk items had been produced in Paisley since 1760.

By the 1820s, when James began making sewing thread, he was a comparatively rich man. He knew something of the process of thread twisting, for one of the elements of crêpe production is the peculiar twist required for the yarn. This process was done for him by Messrs Ross & Duncan, a firm of

I LEARNED MY GREATEST SEWING SECRET FROM THE LAUNDRY BASKET!

"SO OFTEN THINGS I'D SPENT HOURS IN MAKING CAME BACK FROM THE WASH – RUINED! ALL THE COLOR HAD BEEN GRADUALLY DRAINED OUT OF THE THREADS SO THAT STITCHES SHOWED UP AGAINST THE FABRIC!"

"NOW, THANK GOODNESS!, I'VE DISCOVERED A RANGE OF REALLY COLOR-FAST THREADS – COATS' SUPER SHEEN. FROCKS, UNDIES, EVERYTHING I MAKE STAYS LIKE NEW BECAUSE STITCHES NEVER FADE AND SHOW!"

THE nimblest fingers, the nicest materials, the most exacting care —all are discounted unless threads themselves are color-fast! For successful sewing must laugh at laundries. That's why Isobel, the famous British designer of London and Harrogate, says: "I strongly urge the use of Coats' Super Sheen—color-fast . . . because stitches that stay invisible do help garments to stay lovely." Coats' Super Sheen is made in class 40 and 50 for hand and machine sewing.

Use also Milward's "Gold Seal" needles—best for all sewing.

Always ask for...

COLOR-FAST COATS' SUPER SHEEN

Issued by J. & P. Coats Ltd.

FACING PAGE: *Advertisement from the 1890s*
LEFT: *Advertisement in* The Needlewoman, *1935*
BELOW: *Advertisement in* Women's Illustrated, *1952*

the embroidery thread business. There was intense competition between the two firms, but, in 1889, they agreed to form a distributing agency to market their goods, the 'Sewing Cotton Agency', later referred to as 'The Central Agency'. In 1896, a group of companies came together under the name of the then largest member, J & P Coats Ltd.

twiners, whose firm James later entered as a sleeping partner. This gave him the opportunity to learn the business, and, when, in 1826, his contract with them expired, he built a small mill at Ferguslie where he started making thread.

When he retired in 1830, he left the weaving business to his partners and to his son William. He gave the thread business to his sons, James and Peter, which became J & P Coats. They expanded the business and developed a large trade in America. In about 1870, when the Americans imposed a high import duty on finished thread, they were obliged to build mills in the United States. Those at Pawtucket, on Rhode Island, were as large as the Paisley ones.

In 1890, the firm became a limited liability company with a capital of £5.75 million. Paisley was now a thriving town, recognized as the home of thread making, for it was also the home of thread makers, Clark & Company, whose Anchor brand dominated

In 1931 there was a major reorganization of the UK manufacturing to form United Thread Mills Ltd. Thread is not just a commodity but is regarded as a decorative feature of garments and handicrafts, giving rise to embroidery threads such as Stranded Cotton and Pearl Cotton. These and the mercerized sewings are all produced in a wide range of colours.

The Russian Revolution and the Second World War deprived the

J. & P. COATS' THREAD IS STRONG!

company of manufacturing units in such countries as Russia, Poland, Hungary and Czechoslovakia. After the war, new raw materials have emerged, particularly synthetics, and new mills were built in markets such as India and Venezuela.

For many years, both Coats and Clarks products were distributed around the world by The Central Agency but, in 1966, J & P Coats (UK) Ltd was formed to conduct all the company's activities in the United Kingdom, Scandinavia and Finland.

By 1961, Coats had already merged with Patons and Baldwins Limited to form the Coats Patons Group and a further merger took place with Vantona Viyella in 1986 to form Coats Viyella. Today, once again, the company is trading in Eastern Europe.

COATS'
SUPER SHEEN
OVER 250 COLORS - GUARANTEED SUN AND WASH FAST

LEFT: *Advertisement from 1935*
ABOVE: *Advertisement from the turn of the century*

FACING PAGE: *Advertisements and packaging from the 1930s*

Jennifer , Bridget , Frances & Elizabeth Good

Guildford in Surrey started to develop as a market town in the early years of the nineteenth century. Long a coaching town, now with improved roads and the coming of the railway in 1845, it became a buoyant place and at 20 High Street was a small grocer's shop owned by Charles Gates.

We know little of Charles, except that, by 1871, he had become agent for Gilbey's wines and spirits. When he died in 1882, he was succeeded by his two sons, Charles Arthur Gates and Leonard Gates, who the following year were advertising themselves as tea and coffee merchants. Perhaps they decided to change from alcohol to milk, for they changed the name of the business from Gates Groceries to The West Surrey Dairy.

The company bought local milk, installed a milk separator and that same year, 1885, introduced a company label depicting a cow looking over a gate. Now it started selling small brown jugs of cream, the jugs bearing the cow and gate symbol; the separated milk was sold back to farmers to feed pigs and calves, although some was taken out on the milk floats, on late-morning deliveries, as 'pudding milk'.

Charles and Leonard were joined in the firm by brothers Bramwell, Ernest and Stanley, and by Bramwell's son Walter, who joined in 1889, and was company chairman from 1936 to 1957. Creameries were opened

Their Best Friend

The FOOD of the 'QUADS'

between 1887 amd 1895 at Wincanton in Somerset, Sherborne and Beaminster in Dorset, and at Kildorrey in Ireland. Cream was in great demand and was kept sweet and mould-free by adding a very small quantity of boric acid. Any surplus cream was made into butter, which was stored in cellars at Guildford, excavated fifty feet deep in the chalk rock where the temperature was constant. In 1888, the company became the West Surrey Central Dairy Co.

After 1902, the Just-Hatmaker roller drying machine was introduced into England and the following year one was installed at Sherborne. Here the separated milk was dried, packed and sold for baking and the pudding market. Similar equipment was later installed at the company's other premises. In 1904, the Carnegie Laboratory in New York showed the benefits of feeding the poor with dried milk and, about this time, the Medical Officer of Health for Leicester asked the company to supply full-cream powdered milk, and later half-cream powder.

In 1908, the first known advertisement for Cow & Gate milk appeared, in volume 1 of the *Medical Officer,* for Dried Pure *English* Milk. In the same journal were encouraging reports of feeding babies on dried milk, and Cow & Gate was specifically mentioned. The *Guildford Directory* of 1908 had a whole page advertisement for various dried milk products, including Cow & Gate.

Previously, dairy products formed the greater part of the company's activities, but now the babyfood products became increasingly important. In 1910, the company issued a leaflet *Hand Feeding Schedule* about the use of 'Cow & Gate Pure English Milk in Dry Form', which recommended two-hourly day feeds and two feeds during the night for a baby's first three weeks.

The cow looking over the gate was registered as a trademark in 1908, but since that time its appearance has been modified on several occasions; it is said that the gate does not represent the part played by the Gates family.

When Wallen's Dairies at Kilburn was acquired in 1924, this was the company's first venture into the bottled milk business. In 1933, this became Home Counties Dairies Ltd, a subsidiary of Cow & Gate Ltd. As results improved, the production of babyfoods expanded and the 'artificial feeding' of babies became more widespread. Other formulae were introduced to meet special medical needs, including 'Frailac' for

ABOVE: *The original Cow & Gate shop*
LEFT: *Early Cow & Gate symbol*
FACING PAGE, TOP RIGHT: *Advertisement from 1957*
FACING PAGE, BELOW LEFT: *Advertisement from* Festival of Britain Guide, *1951*

premature babies. From 1924, Export Milk Food has been used in the tropics and Cow & Gate has become known all over the warmer parts of the world, although it was not until 1929 that the actual company changed its name to Cow & Gate Ltd. In 1936, two cases of Cow & Gate milk food were sent to India, at the urgent request of a famous maharajah, but it was later discovered it was for use in his riding stables!

In 1930, Cow & Gate registered 'Smiler' as a trademark with the Cow & Gate crown on his head, and the slogan 'The Food of Royal Babies'.

The first set of quads known to survive more than a few days were born to a Mrs Miles of St Neots in 1935 and were fed on 'Frailac' and later on half-cream and then full-cream Cow & Gate babymilk. The directors gave them (and also three other sets of quads brought up on Cow & Gate) a twenty-

Which came first....?

Baby is not in the least bit interested in the classical example of indecision—which came first, the chicken or the egg? She knows nothing of the egg, but she can see the chicken. Although mothers may not give a thought to the vast amount of scientific research and painstaking testing which ensures the perfection of Cow & Gate Milk Food they, like baby, believe the evidence of their own eyes.

How stimulating and encouraging it is for wise mothers who have pinned their faith, like so many Royal Mothers, on Cow & Gate, to watch their babies grow into fine, healthy, happy children with that right royal Cow & Gate look! Cow & Gate Milk Food has been the choice of wise mothers for over half a century—three generations of babies. This coupled with the fact that no less than fourteen Royal Babies have been fed on this "King of foods and food of Kings" must mean something.

Can you do better for your baby? Buy a tin TODAY.

COW & GATE MILK FOOD
The FOOD of ROYAL BABIES

first birthday party at the Grosvenor House Hotel in London in 1956. In 1939, Cow & Gate provided milk for a set of Chinese quads who were all alive several years later.

During the years of the Second World War, dried milk products came under the control of the Ministry of Food, but exports were still welcomed and Smiler was often used to herald supplies, sometimes wearing, instead of a crown, a topee or a tin helmet.

Throughout its history, Cow & Gate has acknowledged that breastmilk is the best food available to a baby, but for those mothers unable to breastfeed, it has endeavoured to provide the best possible alternative. Cow & Gate now also makes a wide selection of baby and junior foods to meet the dietary needs of growing babies and toddlers.

Cow & Gate is now part of Nutricia Ltd.

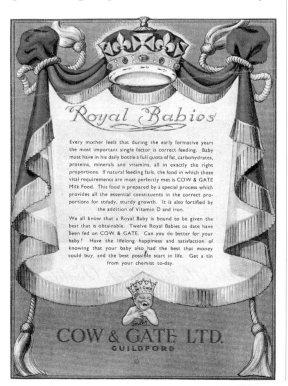

Royal Babies

Every mother feels that during the early formative years the most important single factor is correct feeding. Baby must have in his daily bottle a full quota of fat, carbohydrates, proteins, minerals and vitamins, all in exactly the right proportions. If natural feeding fails, the food in which these vital requirements are most perfectly met is COW & GATE Milk Food. This food is prepared by a special process which provides all the essential constituents in the correct proportions for steady, sturdy growth. It is also fortified by the addition of Vitamin D and iron.

We all know that a Royal Baby is bound to be given the best that is obtainable. Twelve Royal Babies to date have been fed on COW & GATE. Can you do better for your baby? Have the lifelong happiness and satisfaction of knowing that your baby also had the best that money could buy, and the best possible start in life. Get a tin from your chemist to-day.

COW & GATE LTD.
GUILDFORD

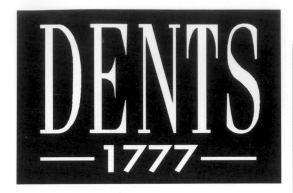

Glove making has been part of the life of Worcester since the thirteenth century; Dents itself has been there for over 200 years.

John Dent was born in 1751 and when he was fourteen he was apprenticed to James Perkins, a master glover, in Worcester. An apprenticeship lasted seven years and, as an apprentice, could not marry, frequent inns, taverns or alehouses, or gamble. He learnt every aspect of the trade, from the treatment of the raw skin to producing the finished glove.

Having completed his apprenticeship, he became a Freeman of the City of Worcester which allowed him to trade within the city. However, he had to sign an oath to the King and Mayor, promising to obey the laws of the country, the bye-laws of the City of Worcester, pay his taxes and, if he took an apprentice, ensure he served the full seven years.

John completed his apprenticeship in 1772 and started in business around 1777. He and his wife Elizabeth lived at 26 Sidbury, Worcester, which was also their manufacturing base, and they had four sons: Benjamin, who became a vicar; Thomas, who died at the age of forty-one; and John jnr and William, who later inherited the business. John Dent also trained a lad, Jeremiah Malcolm Allcroft, whose son joined Dents and, in 1845, purchased the company.

After John Dent's death in 1811, John jnr and William ran the business and trade was good until 1826, when the government lifted the ban on the importation of gloves. This had a serious effect on the glove trade, as the French were able to supply fine quality kid gloves at low prices, and many small firms went out of business.

John and William Dent accepted the challenge, improved the quality of their products, opened a warehouse in London, imported gloves from France and other countries and also started to export their gloves. In 1845, when the brothers retired, twenty-one-year-old John Derby Allcroft bought the business of J & W Dent and continued to trade under that name. In an agreement made in 1852, the firm became

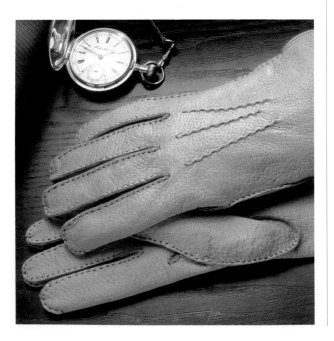

FACING PAGE, TOP: *John Dent, 1751–1811*
FACING PAGE, BELOW: *Today's gloves, still made to the highest quality*
RIGHT: *Grenoble factory, late-nineteenth century*
BELOW: *Early 1930s' shop display stand*

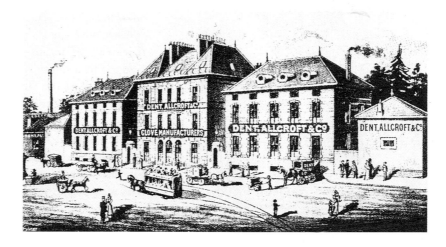

Dent, Allcroft & Co, although since John and William Dent retired the Dent family have not been involved in the business.

As people became more prosperous, gloves were a fashion 'must'. The introduction of production techniques such as webs or knives which could cut out the whole glove, the sewing-machine in 1845 (although not introduced to the glove trade until about 1870), and steam power all had their impact on the industry. The scientific sizing of gloves was also an important innovation. As the company grew, it opened up factories, leather yards and warehouses in New York, Paris, Grenoble, Brussels, Prague, Naples and other centres, making Dents a household name throughout the world.

At home, the company expanded and, in 1853, bought Warmstry House in Palace Yard, Worcester as a factory; it was to be its home for the next 106 years. In a partnership agreement, drawn up in the early 1870s, the partners were bound to distribute annually a percentage of the profits to staff who merited it – an early example of profit-sharing.

Skins were generally received in a half-dressed state, many from Russia and Germany, English skins being regarded as too porous. Most skins came from animals that had been covered with hair rather than

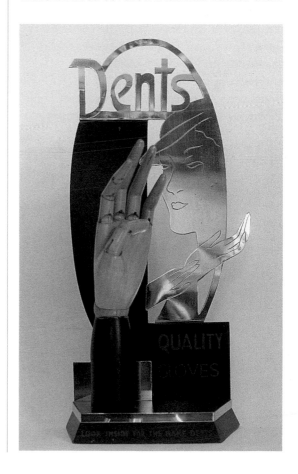

dyed and pared to reduce their thickness. The next stage was to cut them into square pieces the size of a glove, the back and front being in one piece. The gloves were then cut by machine, the decorative stitching on the back was added, and the final sewing of the fingers and closing of the gloves was carried out by most intricate machines – one pair of gloves would go through twenty to thirty pairs of hands!

The devastating effects of two world wars meant that some factories had to close, but 1919 is remembered as the year the famous motto 'Dents hand in glove with the world' was introduced – a phrase used until 1965.

In the late 1950s the glove industry again suffered from cheap imports. Competition came from Taiwan, Korea and the Philippines and, with the introduction of the Europan Free Trade Area, cheap imports also came from Eastern Europe. Although trading conditions were bad in the late 1960s, Dents won the Gold Medallion Export Award by increasing export sales by forty per cent over two years.

A nineteenth-century *Dictionary of Etiquette* states: 'Gloves should be worn by a lady when out walking or driving, at tea dances, balls, dinner parties, the opera or theatre. Men should wear gloves in the street or at a ball, when paying a call, driving, riding, and in church.' Gloves are not worn as much as they were in those elegant times, but Dents still continues to craft its fine leather gloves in the traditional manner. The company is proud of its heritage and of its founder, John Dent.

wool. The dressing was allowed to permeate the skins for several months before they were sorted and washed. They were then dressed with water in which yolk of egg had been mixed, which gave them softness – Dents used several hundred thousand eggs a year for this purpose. The skins were then

Samuel Stern arrived in London from New York in January 1900 with an array of electric speciality gadgets, including illuminated scarf pins, luminous walking sticks for night travellers, a variety of table ornaments, a figure of the Statue of Liberty with a battery-charged Torch of Freedom, illuminated boutonnières (buttonhole flower) and glowing magicians' wands. Each was neatly packaged and indexed in trunks, ready for instant sales display.

He set about his campaign to brighten up London with missionary zeal. He was an extrovert, full of confidence, determined to storm the capital with his 'packaged electricity'. Many people in gas-lit London thought electricity was little more than a novelty – now portable electricity, whatever next? Carrying around electrically-charged appliances might be dangerous, you might be electrocuted in a thunderstorm, or your clothes might be set on fire. Samuel Stern was challenging British conservatism.

FACING PAGE, TOP LEFT: *Hand-cutting leather for gloves*
FACING PAGE, TOP RIGHT: *Shears for cutting leather and glove finger stretchers*
FACING PAGE, BELOW: *A range of modern belts*
RIGHT: *Advertisement in* The Graphic, *1902*
ABOVE: *Batteries were originally hand-made*

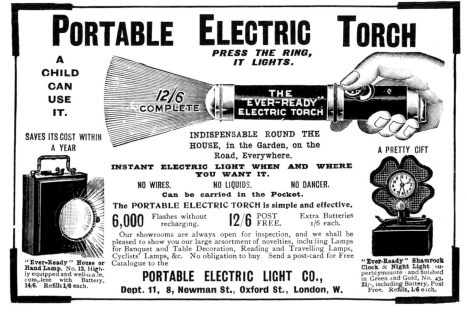

Even if the British public did not want his electrical novelties, he had one line that caught their fancy. It was the simple electric torch which provided 'Instant electric light when and where you want it'. The idea was irresistible, its uses undeniably practical!

Battery manufacturing was, at that time, done by hand, the powder for the cells being mixed in small bowls. The bobbins were rammed by mallets and all the zinc caps were hand-soldered.

Stern was representing the American Electrical Novelty Co of New York, of which he was chairman and had founded in 1898. He approached Mr E B Koopman, Managing Director of the British Mutoscope and Biograph Company,

offering him a concession to market 'Ever Ready Portable Lamps'. The British company was concerned with making and distributing films and, although it had limited resources and marketing experience, the two men drew up a six-month trial trading agreement on 2 March 1900. During that period, the company had to buy not less than £10,000 of Ever Ready goods from America.

Ever Ready's No. 1 Flash Torch flooded the market and sold well, even at twelve shillings each; the quota was fully met and a further agreement was signed to purchase £20,000 of goods over the next twelve months. Ever Ready had established a foothold in Britain.

Quickly, distribution agencies were set up in many of the capital cities of Europe, but Stern feared competition from other European manufacturers. He realized he must establish a British production company with

FACING PAGE, TOP:
Catalogue cover
FACING PAGE, BELOW:
*A selection of early
batteries*
LEFT: *Advertisement
in* Illustrated, *1954*
RIGHT: *All-dry
portable receiver,
designed to give 300
hours' listening time*

displayed cigar lighters, nursery lamps, night lights for invalids, photographic dark room lights, reading lamps, etc, but in pride of place was the 'No. 1' Ever Ready Torch Battery.

An advert in *The Sphere* in 1902 described the torch as being 'particularly useful in country houses, stables, outhouses, cellars'. Stern began mail-order sales and sent illustrated catalogues to thousands of homes throughout Britain. At the end of the first year's trading the tax-free dividends were 150 per cent, rising to 600 per cent the second year.

In 1903, factory premises were leased in north London for battery production. The company had also started using new metal filament bulbs which gave the batteries greater durability, but production methods were primitive, every item being hand-made – mechanization was eighteen years away.

a subsidiary to find retail outlets throughout Britain, and on the Continent.

The American Electrical Novelty and Manufacturing Company Limited was established in November 1901, with Stern as chairman, and with offices at 120 Charing Cross Road, London; in modern terminology it was really a subsidiary of the parent American company. Alfred Loebl, a German with little command of English, was appointed general manager, with a staff of twelve men and a boy. Soon Stern and Loebl established their own selling agency, Portable Electric Light Company, in Shaftsbury Avenue. In the showrooms they

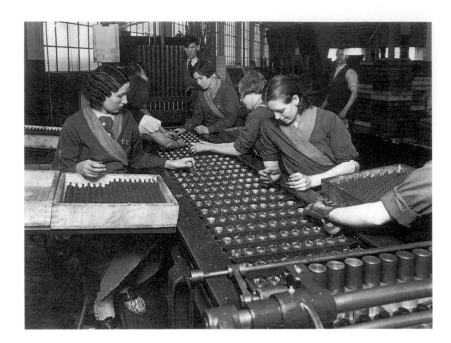

LEFT: *Ever Ready factory c. 1930*
FACING PAGE: *Previously, radios had accumulators which needed recharging*

A major step was taken in 1905, when the company opened a production centre in Sydney, Australia.

On 2 July 1906, the company became the British Ever Ready Electrical Company Limited. 'Ever Ready' was becoming synonymous with torch batteries – the name was bright, alert and had a dependable ring to it. However, the company's main problem was the seasonal demand for its goods – trade and battery production began in June, but slackened off disastrously after Christmas, and staff had to be laid off. Sales drives of non-seasonal items were launched and included dental lamps, battery units for Post Offices and Telegraph services and emergency battery lighting for hospitals.

In 1911, the company moved its offices and factory to the stables of a former horse-drawn tram depot in Hercules Place, Holloway Road, remaining there for over fifty years. An adjoining cinema became an assembly plant.

As sales rose sharply in 1912, the company had a shortage of workers and for the first time employed women – they were more adept than men and they were paid less! Ever Ready was now concentrating on the production of batteries, torch cases, flashlamp cases and motor accessories, as well as the 'double-life' box battery, which used hydrated manganese. These batteries had a grey label figure of Britannia as their trademark. Output of battery cell units exceeded a staggering 15 million, but 1912 was also the year when Alfred Loebl died.

The company was short of capital and, in 1913, it went public. Frederick Gus was appointed chairman at a salary of £14 a week plus one per cent commission on net turnover; Magnus Goodfellow, aged twenty-four, became secretary and director, with a salary of £260 a year and a commission of one-tenth of one per cent on net turnover. Gus was knowledgeable about factory management and battery production; Goodfellow, an accountant, had an uncanny ability with money matters. They learned from each other and made a formidable team. Again, extra production capacity was needed and they took premises in Font Hill Road, Finsbury Park.

With the outbreak of the First World War, many employees left to join the armed forces, resulting in depleted worklines and initial confusion, but soon the existing staff and new women employees were producing batteries for the war effort. New types of batteries were required, some being up to 600 volts. The end of the war brought different problems – over-staffing and a return to seasonal demands – but it also brought the opportunity to establish a research laboratory.

In 1920 the company was again relaunched in a bid for more capital, becoming the Ever Ready Company (Great Britain) Ltd. In September 1920 it made its first take-over bid, acquiring Ecko Battery.

The development of radio stations in 1922 heralded the age of the battery accumulator receiver sets; the 'cat's whisker' had gone. Later, the HT dry battery was used until mains-electricity sets were introduced in 1926. Goodfellow, however, was strengthening Ever Ready's position by acquiring other companies or buying holdings in them.

The company emerged from the General Strike unscathed. By 1927, Ever Ready was the largest battery manufacturer in Europe. In 1928, Magnus Goodfellow became chairman; his prime task was to make the company more self-sufficient by manufacturing its core materials and components. He toured the United States, saw their factory management systems and returned to rationalize Ever Ready's plants. By 1936, his aims were nearly complete, but another war was on the horizon.

Everyone now knew they needed their 'No. 8', the famous Ever Ready electric torch battery torches which were the nation's eyes after dark. Over 20 million were produced during the first year of the war, and by 1942 this had risen to over 54

Naturally... IT GOES ANYWHERE

Women find Ever Ready Alldry Radio a blessing because it can be taken from room to room, indoors or outdoors, and be ready to entertain wherever it is carried. As it needs no aerial, earth or mains wires and uses dry batteries only, Ever Ready Alldry Radio is completely mobile and very much the "housewives choice."

The Ever Ready Type "K", ready to switch on, costs only £15.7.8. Other models available.

EVER READY
MADE IN BRITAIN

A L L D R Y   R A D I O

MADE BY THE MAKERS OF BRITAIN'S BEST BATTERIES

million. Some Ever Ready factories were destroyed by enemy action, others badly damaged, but they kept pace with demands.

In the post-war years, Ever Ready had to acquire new factories and install modern equipment to give it automation; it had to rebuild its overseas markets and once again produce the raw materials needed for self-sufficiency. By 1950, production had been centralized into twelve factories and the labour force reduced from 12,000 to 7,000, but Magnus Goodfellow had died in 1949 and did not live to see his plans completed. To facilitate overseas trade, Berec International was formed as the export division of Ever Ready; in 1960, the value of dry battery exports was £7 million.

The Berec Group, now known as British Ever Ready was purchased by Hanson plc for £95 million in January 1982. Ten years later the business of Ever Ready Limited was purchased by Ralston Purina Company, reuniting the British and US arms of the original company.

fILOFAX

No doubt many people feel that the Filofax is a development of the yuppie 1980s but its origins actually go back to the 1920s.

During the First World War, Colonel Disney, a British Army officer, was working in the United States and came across a form of 'organizer', called the Lefax system, a specialized folder which contained sheets of paper with information which was primarily of interest to technical users, engineers and scientists. The business had been established by a Mr Parker, a Canadian, in Philadelphia in the early years of the twentieth century. Colonel Disney felt the system was so useful, so adaptable and elegant, that it would succeed in Britain. William Rounce, a friend in England, ran a printing company, but also had other interests in stationery and small item manufacturing.

Rounce came to an agreement with Mr Parker to import and distribute Lefax and, in 1921, along with a stationer Posseen Hill, set up a company called Norman & Hill Ltd – the 'Norman' was William Rounce's young son. They opened for business in one small office in Appold Street in the City of London, with only a temporary secretary, Grace Scurr, but she was a remarkable woman.

Grace Scurr was not quite thirty years old when she joined Norman & Hill Ltd.

Today we would say she was good at marketing. She made tremendous efforts to ensure the new product became well known among users, members of the armed services and clergymen – and it was Grace, in 1925, who coined the word 'Filofax'.

Prior to the Second World War, there was not much demand for such a system as life was more leisurely – or those in positions of responsibility had assistants to organize their day – but soon journalists, medical practitioners and lawyers became users, and also told their friends the advantages of the Filofax.

In the early years of the Second World War, London suffered badly from enemy bombings and, on the night of 30 December

FACING PAGE, TOP: *Grace Scurr, aged thirty-three*
FACING PAGE, BELOW: *Grace's old binder*
RIGHT: *A modern Filofax*

1940, the office of Norman & Hill Ltd was destroyed. As Grace Scurr made her way to work the next morning, she found that a hundred yards from the building, barriers, piles of rubble and fires blocked her way. She told the air-raid warden that she wanted to go to her office, but he replied, 'It's all gone, Miss, you've lost everything, that's the end of you.' Opening her handbag she said, 'Oh no it's not. It's all in here. Goodbye.'

In her handbag was her own Filofax; each day she had updated her records, each night she had taken the Filofax home with her. It was safe and so were the company's records. She found temporary offices in Watford and, although it took her three months to get a telephone installed, she then used her Filofax as a source of information to enable her to contact her customers, to tell them the company was still in business and could take their orders. Perhaps she told her customers of her own experience, and how the Filofax had saved her company and might save theirs. Her company? Yes, for the temporary secretary became the company chairman!

In the 1950s, when Grace Scurr retired, the Filofax was still relatively unknown for it had never been widely advertised. In 1959, David Collischon, a marketing executive with Collins publishers, bought himself a Filofax and immediately realized its potential, with its adaptability and its usefulness. Fifteen years later, David and his wife, Lesley, established their own small company called Pocketfax, to act as a wholesaler for Norman & Hill Ltd. They sold the Filofax very successfully by mail-order to the business market and, in 1980, when the owners were considering retiring, David and Lesley bought Norman & Hill Ltd.

David Collischon redesigned the range of materials and made the Filofax even more versatile. He introduced the new company logo, with the use of the now familiar lowercase 'f', followed by the rest of the word in capitals. The name of Filofax was promoted and within six years the turnover of the company had increased 160-fold – a remarkable growth. The Filofax had become a cult symbol.

It is said that David and Lesley paid £10,000 for the company. When it was floated on the stock exchange in 1987 it was worth £17 million. In 1988, the turnover was £14.7 million with a record profit of £2.72 million. The Collischons had become very rich.

The developing recession caused a major turn-round in the company's fortunes as Filofax had to compete with cheaper imitations. In November 1990, the share price dropped to an all-time low of 13p and a new management team was brought in to revitalize Filofax. The man to play a major part in this revival was Robin Field, who later became chief executive.

Today, Filofax is to be found throughout the world, but few know of Grace Scurr and her story.

Fisher-Price

Herman Guy Fisher was born in 1898 in Unionville, Pennsylvania, USA and, although his father died when Herman was only five years old, he went on to study commerce and marketing at college. To enable him to attend college, he took jobs as a brush seller, in a clothing store, in a steel mill and even as an usher at a local theatre. On graduating, it was difficult to find work and eventually he moved to Rochester, New York where, in 1926, he got a job with a company specializing in paper boxes and games, the Alderman-Fairchild Company. Later, the company split into two parts, launching All-Fair Toys.

All-Fair Toys moved to Churchville, New York, where Fisher became vice-president and general manager. All-Fair's slogan was 'Our Work is Child's Play', a slogan later bought by Fisher-Price for a nominal sum. Fisher, along with a group of investors, made an unsuccessful attempt to purchase All-Fair in 1930, but as a result of this, and with encouragement from Elbert Hubbard II and Irving Price, a new toy company, Fisher-Price Toys, was formed that year in East Aurora, New York. The founding partners were Herman Fisher, Irving Price and Helen Schelle. Irving Price had been a senior manager for F W Woolworth & Co and became the financial backer of the partnership, whilst Helen Schelle had invaluable experience in the retail toy industry. Herman Fisher was president and general manager, Irving Price became treasurer and chairman of the board of directors, and Helen Schelle was secretary and treasurer, the executive responsible for the book-keeping, financial activities and sale of stock.

Price and his wife had thirty-six per cent ownership of the company, Fisher twenty-four per cent, Schelle five per cent, and a few mainly local people also had a stake in the firm. Soon a 7,500 square foot factory

FACING PAGE, TOP: *Herman Fisher*
FACING PAGE, BELOW: *'Chatter telephone'*
LEFT: *Irving Price*
RIGHT: *Helen Schelle*

was acquired and, particularly using Helen Schelle's expertise, they designed toys in which 'the shape, expression, and colour immediately captured the child's attention' – they found little of that 'magic' in existing toys. Irving Price's wife, Margaret, who was an illustrator and writer of children's books, helped in the design of the toys. It was said that the designs were 'a step forward in the toy industry'.

The early growth of the company was slow; two-thirds of the capital was lost between 1930 and 1934, but the toys gradually became popular. Fisher developed a five-point creed for the business. Toys must have:

1. Intrinsic play value
2. Ingenuity
3. Strong construction
4. Good value for the money
5. Action

The creed also stated: 'Children love best the cheerful, friendly toys with amusing action, toys that appeal to their imagination, toys that DO something new and surprising and funny. This idea is so simple it is sometimes overlooked – but if you have forgotten your own younger days, test it out on the nearest children.' Fisher stated: 'We design our toys to look and act like toys should.'

In the early days, the firm's fifteen employees often only worked a three-day week, but this was increased to a full five days when expansion took place. The majority of the jobs were done by hand and the assembly line was simply a long table where the toys were put together. Quality control meant one employee checked another, and made any necessary corrections; indeed, the first 149 toys were thrown out because their quality was not acceptable to Herman Fisher.

Overflow work was done by local families on a piecework basis but, as parents often made their children do the work, this was stopped when the child labour laws were enforced, and the work was contracted to Goodwill Industries, a firm employing handicapped workers. Most of an early successful range of toys, the Pop-Up Kritters, had to be discontinued in 1934 as they proved too expensive to manufacture, but, as mechanization was introduced, costs dropped dramatically and some were re-introduced.

High-quality Ponderosa pine, a fine, close-grained timber, was used as it did not splinter and was light in weight. It was transported 2,500 miles, from the west, to the factory. The toys were decorated with permanently laminated lithographs and brass eyelets were used to prevent wear as the axles spun.

Creating 'action toys' was a high priority and bellows were added to produce 'quacks' and 'barks'; bells also contributed to the

toys' noise appeal. A catalogue was produced which gave details of toys such as Drummer Bear, Bark Puppy, Woodsy-Wee Circus, Dizzy Dino, and at the New York City Toy Fair, in 1931, the 'Sixteen Hopefuls' were unveiled. 700 stores, including Macy's in New York City, sold Fisher-Price toys in 1931.

In 1932, Herman Fisher gained a controlling interest in the company and, in 1933, made his first international sale, to Harrods. In 1934, the first pre-school range was introduced. It wasn't until 1936, when the company made 100,000 toys, that it first came into profit – $3,000 on sales of $250,000. In 1937, with the end of the Great Depression, two million toys were produced; by the autumn of 1938 it could not keep up with demand, and a night shift had to be introduced. The particular new star was Snoopy Sniffer. It was designed by Edward Savage, often described as a 'natural inventor', who created the 'Wobble idea', used in the 'Go 'n' Nack Jumbo', which swayed from side-to-side as it walked; the mechanism was designed so that the animal moved backwards and forwards at random. Snoopy Sniffer sold almost 4.5 million from 1938 to 1964.

By 1940, the firm had three assembly lines, each with two shifts, three sales representatives, a new fabrication department and the beginnings of an engineering department.

After the war, in the 1950s, Fisher-Price began to experiment with plastic: a cleaner, safer and more flexible material – it transformed toy design.

In the 1970s the company grew dramatically after being purchased by the Quaker Oats Company, a company with a similar management philosophy to Fisher-Price.

In the United Kingdom, a factory was established at Peterlee, County Durham, where research took place to develop toys for older children. Today, its toys are sold all over Europe and, in Britain, one child in every two plays with a Fisher-Price activity toy. In 1989, Fisher-Price acquired Kiddicraft toys, a leading pre-school toy manufacturer.

In 1991, Fisher-Price became an independent, publicly traded company, on the New York stock exchange, but is now part of Mattel. Today Fisher-Price toys are sold in nearly a hundred countries. Its most popular toy is still the Chatter Telephone – over 30 million have been sold since it was introduced in 1957.

ABOVE: *'Rocka-Stack'*
BELOW: *Best-selling pull-along dog*

FACING PAGE, LEFT: *The now familiar packaging*
FACING PAGE, RIGHT: *Fisherman's Friend contributed to Blackpool Illuminations and the illuminated tram*

FISHERMAN'S FRIEND

James Lofthouse was born in Lancaster, but soon afterwards the family moved a few miles south to the fishing port of Fleetwood. Here, in 1865, he opened his pharmacy and chemist's shop where local trawlermen came to seek relief from their bronchial

ailments, acquired in the freezing fog and frosty conditions of the north Atlantic fishing grounds. Determined to help his fishermen friends, he set to work to develop a remedy and, after much experimentation, he created an extra-strong formula.

At first, the remedy was offered as a liquid preparation, but the bottles were easily broken in the rough and tumble as the giant waves beat against the small fishing vessels. Next, he created lozenges, stamped out of a thick dough, enriched with liquorice, capsicum, eucalyptus and menthol. The menthol-enriched lozenges proved to be an ideal remedy for the throat and chest complaints suffered by the fishing folk and soon news of

their effectiveness was passed from one to another across the local fishing community.

Customers constantly came and asked for either 'a bag of fisherman's lozenges' or 'an ounce of friends' – there was no need to invent a brand name. Fisherman's Friend had been born. Only rarely would a trawler leave the port without someone having a supply of the lozenges about their person; only rarely would the local folk not have one of James Lofthouse's little white envelopes, filled with the lozenges, in their medicine cupboard.

Fisherman's Friend was a well-kept secret by that local community for almost a century. It was in 1963 that the wonders of James Lofthouse's remedy started to spread outside Fleetwood, and it now reaches the far corners of the world. Doreen Lofthouse, wife of Tony, grandson of the founder, along with her mother-in-law Frances, realized the potential of the old recipe and took to the road. They travelled across Lancashire, selling the lozenges direct to retailers, and soon found a ready response in both town and country. It was even suggested they came just in time to ease the sore throats of the screaming Beatles fans!

By 1969, the demand had become so great that it was no longer practical to pack and distribute the product from the rear of

the tiny pharmacy where James Lofthouse had first evolved his recipe; a new venue had to be found. They discovered in Fleetwood a disused tram shed which was brought into use, but even this proved to be inadequate for the company's needs and within two years the family were negotiating the purchase of land in Maritime Street, Fleetwood.

When the new 20,000 square foot factory was opened in 1972, the company still only employed eight full-time staff. They believed that their expansion would now be complete, but still the British market grew and so did their overseas sales. They also expanded the product range to include other varieties of lozenge and a honey cough syrup.

In recent years, Fisherman's Friend has been endorsed at London's Guy's Hospital and by leading politicians, including Margaret Thatcher, who value the way the lozenges ease throats exposed to too much public speaking. Both Chris Bonnington, on his Everest expedition, and the crew of the yacht *Challenger*, when they took part in the round-the-world race, carried supplies of Fisherman's Friend to ease them on their way.

Today, its markets stretch from Japan to Sweden, from Canada to Australia. Back in Fleetwood, in a complex of buildings which now covers 100,000 square feet, a replica of the original tiny pharmacy has been re-created.

Tony Lofthouse is now company chairman and Doreen Lofthouse is managing director of a company which produces 1,000 million lozenges a year! In the days of hand production, output rarely exceeded 6,000 lozenges a day, but with today's automated systems it is normal to produce 400,000 lozenges an hour.

Goddard's

Joseph Goddard was born at Market Harborough, the son of a local banker. He went to London to train as a chemist and, on his return, bought a shop in Gallowtree Gate in Leicester. As most chemists did, he made and sold a lot of his own medicines, perhaps his most successful one being a cure for foot-rot in sheep.

Joseph was also an entrepreneur and found a niche in the market with a new product for cleaning silver. In 1833, Michael Faraday had published the results of research he had done into electrolysis, and soon afterwards the first silver-plated spoons and forks were made, replacing the commonly used steel cutlery. Goddard saw his chance. He realized that the mercurial polish usually used to clean silver would soon wear away the thin layer of plated silver and so he decided to create a cleaning material that was harmless to the silver and to the user. The preparation had to be softer than the silver and yet hard enough to remove tarnish; it also had to polish the silver and give it a pleasing mellow gleam.

Soon he came up with his alternative which he called Goddard's Non-Mercurial Plate Powder. At first, it was only sold in his own chemist's shop, but, as it became better known, he invited agents who called at his shop to try the polish, and then take it and sell it to other retailers. In a few years his product was in use throughout the country.

Goddard decided to sell his chemist's shop and concentrate all his efforts on the polish. He was joined by his son, Joseph

Wallis Goddard, who had been apprenticed to Sir Gilbert Scott, a noted architect, and young Joseph used his early training to good effect by designing a new factory for the family firm.

Joseph Goddard died in 1877 and his son continued to expand the business. The country was experiencing a time of prosperity and, as silver grew in popularity, so did the need for their product, which had no competitors.

Joseph W Goddard was a clever and energetic businessman, a keen Baptist, a non-smoker and a vegetarian. He was responsible for opening the first vegetarian establishment in Leicester; he also gave land for tennis courts, but only on the strict understanding that they were not to be used on Sundays. He was a great believer in the power of advertising and used it to good effect.

FACING PAGE, TOP: *James Lofthouse's chemist shop*
FACING PAGE, BELOW: *Feature in 1989 Spanish magazine*

RIGHT: *Advertisement in* The Strand, *1948*

Gives more time for other things..

QUICK..
EASY..
LASTING..

Goddard's
SILVER POLISH

also Plate Powder, Furniture Cream,
Brass Polish and Shoe Polishes

It was not until the First World War that the monopoly of his product was challenged. He met the challenge head on by the introduction of new products such as a liquid silver polish.

The third generation of Goddards now took charge of the firm and they employed James Thornton, an industrial chemist, to develop new products. His first success was a furniture cream, and, as others followed, it became necessary, in 1933, to build a spacious new factory in Nelson Street, Leicester.

During the Second World War, the company continued to prosper, even though it lost many of its export markets. Goddard's created specialist polishes for use in aircraft manufacture and in precision engineering. Very important to the servicemen and women was the development of a button polish which, if spilt, left no mark on the uniform, and also a white dressing for web belts, which was a solid material, brilliant white, and did not rub off. They also developed a polish for the plastic windows and windshields of aircraft; in peacetime this led to the creation of anti-static cloths for use in the photographic, television and record industries.

After the war, fewer homes had servants to clean silver and Goddard's research team looked for a simple, safe way of doing the task; in 1953, they introduced Silver Dip in the Leicester area. It was an immediate success following a national advertising campaign linked to in-store demonstrations. Now it was possible to dip cutlery in the jar, rinse, and all stains had gone and the cutlery was ready for use. The Wax Polish Department also had new ideas, introducing Silicone Wax and Creamed Silicone Wax polishes in 1954. Later products included Long Term Silver Polish, Long Term Silver Foam and the Long Term Silver Polishing Cloth, and, for stainless steel, Goddard's Stainless Steel Care.

Links were created between Goddard's and S C Johnson, of Wisconsin in the United States. Both were family businesses, both run by the great-grandson of the founder, and both involved in the supply of domestic polishes. In 1969, Goddard's became a totally owned subsidiary of Johnson Wax Ltd.

LEFT: *Edwardian advertisement*
ABOVE: *From the* Trade Marks Journal, *1895*

FACING PAGE, TOP: *Emile Berliner*
FACING PAGE, BELOW: *Nipper, facing the gramophone*

KNOW HMV · KNOW MUSIC

In 1887, Emile Berliner, a Hanover-born American immigrant, filed Letters Patent in the United States for his 'Gramophone' method of recording and reproducing sound. He had devised a method of recording onto flat discs, tracing 'voice patterns' onto a heavy glass disc coated with an inky mixture of oil and lamp-black, which was then fixed with shellac and photo-engraved into a flat metal disc. He also devised a new machine to play the discs; the name 'Gramophone' was an inversion of the name Edison had given to his tin foil recordings, 'Phonograms'. Two years later, his hand-operated gramophones were exported from Germany, where a European pressing plant had been established, to Britain, but it was not until 1895 that the 'Berliner Gramophone Company' was formed in California. The records at that time were made from vulcanized rubber.

Ten years after Berliner had filed his Letters Patent in America, William Barry Owen, a director of the National Gramophone Company in New York, arrived in Britain to exploit the Berliner Gramophone patents. He resigned from the American company and set up his business base at the Hotel Cecil in London.

In 1897, William Barry Owen and Trevor Williams formed the Gramophone Company. They made arrangements to manufacture gramophone records and 'assemble' the gramophone machines in Germany. Fred Gaisberg, a young recording engineer and talent scout, who had previously worked for Berliner in America, also came to London to be the company's first recording engineer. For one of his first British recordings, he got Syria Lamonte, a barmaid at Rules restaurant in Maiden Lane, Covent Garden, to sing 'Coming Thru' the Rye'. The now famous 'Recording Angel' trademark was devised for the company by Theodore Birnbaum and started to appear on its records.

A new process had been developed for the manufacture and duplication of sound recordings based on cutting the master recording into a wax blank; the Gramophone Company purchased the rights to use this process in Europe and throughout the British Empire.

LEFT: *The familiar label of millions of gramophone records*
BELOW: *Francis Barraud*
FACING PAGE, TOP: *Early delivery van*
FACING PAGE, BELOW: *The HMV shop in London's Oxford Street in the early 1920s.*

Whilst all these developments were taking place, Francis Barraud, a photographer and artist, had taken a photograph in Liverpool of his brother's pet dog, Nipper. Nipper was a 'keen ratter' we are told and lost an eye during a battle with a rodent. The dog died in 1895 but it was not until 1898 that the artist, Barraud, painted the dog, working from the photograph. He faced the dog, listening to a phonograph. Later Barraud wrote, 'It suddenly occurred to me that to have the dog listening to the phonograph, with an intelligent and rather puzzled expression, and call it His Master's Voice, would make an excellent subject . . . it was certainly the happiest thought I ever had.'

On 31 May 1899, Barraud visited the Gramophone Company and left a photograph of the painting. On 15 September, he received an offer of £100: £50 for the picture and £50 for a transfer of the copyright of the picture, conditional on Barraud painting out the phonograph and painting in a gramophone provided by the company. The altered picture was completed in less than three weeks and, on 31 January 1900, the copyright was assigned to the Gramophone Company, with the words 'His Master's Voice', although they were not used at that time.

That same year, the Gramophone Company's sales representative set sail for Australia with 100,000 records. Later that year, it started making recordings using the new wax process and also gained rights to manufacture the Lambert typewriter, the company becoming the Gramophone and Typewriter Ltd.

Over the next few years Nipper appeared on needle boxes and promotional literature, but did not appear on the British company's headed paper until 1907, and it wasn't until 1911 that the words 'His Master's Voice' became the official trademark, although it had been used on a record label in 1909.

In 1902, Enrico Caruso, the great operatic singer, made his first records in Milan. He recorded ten songs for a fee of £100, the records all being made in the space of two hours in one afternoon.

Her Majesty Queen Alexandra granted the company its first Royal Warrant in 1907, the same year that Edward Lloyd, a famous tenor, cut the first sod, and Madame (later Dame) Nellie Melba laid the foundation stone at the Hayes factory site. In 1910,

when Captain Scott and his party went to the Antarctic, they were given a gramophone and records to take with them – this gramophone was later brought back to England and is now part of the company's archives.

Although the factory at Hayes was well equipped with the latest facilities, soundproof rooms were not very effective and so the company bought all the chickens in the vicinity to prevent their cackling being picked up by the recording apparatus.

In 1921, the Gramophone Company opened its new store in London's Oxford Street and, there above the doors, was the name HMV. The premises were opened by Sir Edward Elgar. Soon the gramophone record was used to present messages to the nation. George V and Queen Mary recorded messages to the boys and girls of the Empire in 1923, and, in 1924, the Gramophone Company recorded the King's speech at the opening of the Wembley Exhibition, using a wireless loudspeaker, connected by a short tube to the recording box. Electrical recording commenced in 1925, when the company made its first recording of a church organ using a land line to link to the recording equipment.

The Gramophone Company Ltd and the Columbia Graphophone Company Ltd merged in 1931, the year that Sir Edward Elgar opened the new EMI Recording Studios in Abbey Road in London. George V's first Christmas broadcast to the Empire, in 1932, was recorded by HMV.

The Decca Record Company launched the 33rpm microgroove long-playing record in Britain in 1950. Two years later, EMI introduced its first 33rpm, as well as introducing the 7-inch 45rpm single records, these being followed by the 7-inch mono-extended-play records. Stereo 7.5ips reel-to-reel pre-recorded tapes, stereo LPs, and stereo extended play 7-inch 45rpm records soon followed. The last EMI 78rpm record was recorded in 1960; it featured Russ Conway playing 'Rule Britannia' and 'Royal Event'.

In 1962, EMI formed the World Record Club Ltd and Music For Pleasure, jointly with Paul Hamlyn, and, in 1969, introduced pre-recorded stereo eight-track cartridges. For a long time Electric & Musical Industries had been known as EMI; now it became EMI Records Ltd.

Towards the end of the 1970s, Thorn Electrical Industries made a take-over bid for EMI – the offer was £148 million. In 1992, EMI Music acquired Richard Branson's Virgin Records. There are now almost 100 HMV stores in the United Kingdom, including the world's largest music store in London's Oxford Street. HMV is an autonomous company within the EMI Group plc, the United Kingdom's premier music, video and games retailer.

Number 77 Copperas Hill, Liverpool had connections with two major railway projects: Frank Hornby, creator of the Hornby Railway system was born there in 1863, and secondly, ironically, it was demolished for the building of Lime Street Station.

Frank was one of the seven children of provision dealer John Hornby and his wife, Martha. He married Clara Godfroy in 1887, and they had three children, Roland Godfroy, Douglas Egerton and Patricia Elliott. Although Frank worked as a book-keeper and cashier for a meat importer, and became chief managing clerk, he spent much of his spare time inventing things, a hobby stemming from childhood.

One of the first books Frank had been given when a young boy, *Self-Help* by Samuel Smiles, told the stories of famous inventors, and outlined the difficulties they faced before they reached success. It had a lasting influence on him. The story that fascinated him most was of Palissy, who invented a white glaze for earthenware, but had many failures on the way. Deciding to be an inventor was one thing; how to set about it

ABOVE: *1932* Meccano Magazine
LEFT: *Instructions for an early Meccano set*
FACING PAGE, ABOVE: Hornby Book of Trains 1937–8
FACING PAGE, BELOW: *1959* Meccano Magazine

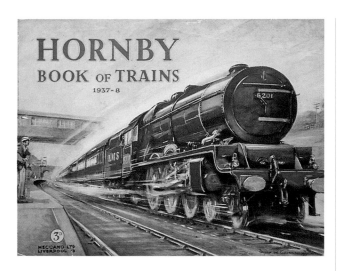

was another. He thought he might develop a machine to solve the problem of perpetual motion. Through experiments and study of the principles of mechanics, he learned many skills, but had to abandon the project and turn to other ideas, such as a submarine which, when placed on the water, submerged itself, was propelled for some distance under water, but then, alas, failed to re-emerge. He lacked adequate tools in his small workshop, but was never discouraged, especially when he remembered James Watt and his difficulties.

As he gradually accumulated more tools, his ideas turned to interchangeable parts which could be used for a variety of purposes – here was the germ of the Meccano system.

After he and his wife Clara had boys of their own, he delighted in making mechanical toys for them. One Christmas Eve, during a long train journey, he thought of his workshop and the problem he had in getting small parts for a crane they were constructing. Later he wrote, 'I felt that what was required were parts that could be applied in different ways to many different models, and that could be adjusted to give a variety of movements by alteration of position, etc.

In order to do this it was necessary to devise some standard method of fitting one part to any other part; gradually there came to me the conception of parts all perforated with a series of holes of the same size and at the same distance apart. Such parts I realized could be bolted up to a model in different positions and at different angles, and having done their work in one model could be unbolted and applied to another.'

Gradually his ideas clarified, but little did he think that they would change the rest of his life, and result in a hobby that would give hours of pleasure to boys of all ages, in all parts of the world. Enthusiastically, he started to put his ideas into practice, first making strips from a large sheet of copper, which was soft and easy to work. He decided that all the strips would be half an inch

Superb detail and super strength

You will find something more than just realistic reproduction in Hornby-Dublo Electric Trains. Every part is accurately made in solid metal to give lasting strength. A thrilling system operated by remote control can be set out on the table. Ask your dealer for the new Hornby-Dublo coloured folder, or write direct to Meccano Limited, Binns Road, Liverpool 13.

'Silver King' is one of the powerful 'Pacific' type express locomotives operated by British Railways. The valve gear and other details are attractively reproduced in this magnificent Hornby-Dublo model.

Made and Guaranteed by Meccano Ltd.

HORNBY DUBLO ELECTRIC TRAINS

wide, with equal-sized holes along the centre at half-inch intervals. At first he made a two-and-a-half-inch strip, then a five-and-a-half-inch, and so on, up to twelve-and-a-half-inch which seemed to him an enormous part. The measurements have never been changed since. Similarly, he had to make his own nuts and bolts, and his own angle brackets, axles and wheels – it was a long job, but it was a great day for Frank and his boys when they assembled their first Meccano crane. He was so sure his system was good, he consulted a patent agent and obtained an English patent on 9 January 1901; foreign patents followed.

It was originally called 'Mechanics Made Easy' and was marketed by Hornby and his employer, D H Elliott, trading as Elliott & Hornby from 18 James Street, Liverpool. The trademark Meccano was registered in 1907 and Elliott & Hornby was sold to Meccano Ltd in 1908, Hornby becoming a director. In 1914, Meccano Ltd moved to a purpose-designed factory at the famous Binns Road, Liverpool 13 address, the company's home until 1979.

In 1916, Hornby launched the monthly *Meccano Magazine*, which was followed by the worldwide fellowship of Meccano boys, the Meccano Guild. Over the years, Meccano sets were introduced, each set converting by

means of an Extension Pack into the next larger sized set. Eventually, there were over 300 individual Meccano parts. Hornby Clockwork trains arrived in 1920, electric ones in 1925. Other products followed, including speedboats, aeroplane and car constructor outfits and Dinky Toys, which were launched in 1933. The Hornby Railway Company was formed for model railway enthusiasts, to run on similar lines to the Meccano Guild.

Frank Hornby stood as a Unionist candidate for Everton in the 1931 General Election and won the seat. By the next election, his health was failing and he did not re-contest the seat. When he died in September 1936, aged seventy-three, he was a millionaire. He was succeeded as chairman by his son Roland. This was the company's golden era – Meccano O gauge railway, Dinky Toys, and many more! In 1938 the smaller OO gauge model railway, known as Hornby Dublo, was introduced.

After the Second World War, production resumed at pre-war levels, but, by 1964, model railway manufacturers were experiencing a recession and Meccano, including Hornby trains, was taken over by Lines Bros Ltd. They merged their own Tri-ang Railways with the Meccano Hornby range and it was renamed Tri-ang Hornby, with production centred at Margate. In 1971, Lines Bros Ltd ceased trading and the Hornby side was bought by Dunbee Combex Marx Ltd, a leading British toy manufacturer, while the Meccano side was bought by Airfix Ltd. Although it has changed hands several times since, Meccano is still made at a factory in Calais, France. Today Hornby Hobbies Ltd still trades from Margate, and now includes other famous brands.

ABOVE: *1953 advertisement*

FACING PAGE: *1967 advertisement*

H U S H   P U P P I E S ®

Jim Muir, the sales manager of Wolverine, a United States shoe company, went on holiday in one of the southern states of North America, where he came across a local food made from small fried corn dough balls, called Hush Puppies. He asked why the dough balls were called Hush Puppies and was told that the farmers used the food to quieten their barking dogs. Jim thought this was a great name for a new style of shoe his company were producing – colloquially, hurting feet were known as barking dogs. A new brand name had been born.

The shoe that Wolverine was introducing was a very simple design with a tan pigskin upper and a light-weight blown-rubber sole, later regarded as the origin of the casual shoe. The only other casual shoes were either trainers or an engineer boot.

In the late 1950s, due to increased mechanization in the United States, there was a move away from labouring jobs to white-collar office work. People had increased prosperity and additional leisure time and Hush Puppies were considered to be the ideal leisure shoe as they were casual, comfortable and 'breathed'. They were launched nationally in the United States in 1958 and within two months were selling across the country. Wolverine had become the market leader in the casual footwear market.

In the United Kingdom, Hush Puppies were introduced by Saxone. By late 1962, Saxone had become part of the British Shoe Corporation and Hush Puppies became one of Britain's best-known shoe brands.

In the early 1990s Hush Puppies were revitalized and promoted, using advertisements which featured several different dogs, all of whom were at ease with their owners; all had the caption 'Be Comfortable With Who You Are'. Hush Puppies shoe shops were opened in high streets and shopping centres. Now, Hush Puppies have become highly fashionable again, and celebrities from Europe and America have been spotted wearing the original casual shoe. The doggy idea has come a long way.

Wish they made Hush Puppies for me– they're so comfortable!

Hush Puppies comfort comes in a wide range of styles. Made from breathing brushed pigskin. Hush Puppies are light, flexible and so caressingly comfortable you hardly know you've got them on. Choose the style that suits you best – and find out what Hush Puppies comfort really means.

JANINE 79/11

Hush Puppies® BRAND

For men, women and children (*lucky dogs*)

Janet Reger

Janet Phillips was born a few years before the Second World War in the East End of London. When the Blitz started, the family moved to Reading. As a child Janet loved playing with paper dolls, dressing them in her own creations. She also loved dressing up in her mother's evening dresses and high-heeled shoes and, best of all, putting on precious lingerie, kept in tissue paper and hardly ever worn!

Janet did not enjoy school; she wanted to get on with growing up. Her father bought

waste fabric, mainly offcuts of rayon so small that all Janet's mother could make from them were bras, which sold in large quantities to Littlewoods. Based on his success with bras, he suggested that Janet should go to Leicester College of Art and Technology to study corsetry and underwear design. She liked clothes, was good at art, and most of all wanted to escape from home. Yes, she would give it a try!

At college her career as a designer was greatly influenced by Mrs Redlich who taught her that designs must be fresh and original, combining style and fit with practicality and comfort. It is a pity Janet did not like book-keeping and business skills, as they would have stood her in good stead in later years. From the start, she designed co-ordinated garments, especially underwear, something unheard of at that time. For her final diploma she presented a matching set of bra, panties and suspender belt with inset panels and olive green embroidery.

When she left college Janet knew she *must* be in London, which her mother agreed with, but for different reasons: Janet could live at home, find a nice Jewish boy and settle down! She worked in Margaret Street, in the heart of the 'rag trade', but later Mrs Redlich told her of a job with Daintyfit, a bra manufacturer. However, Janet was restless and, before long, she had

FACING PAGE, ABOVE: *Peter and Janet Reger in the early 70s* FACING PAGE, BELOW: *From the 1972 collection* LEFT AND BELOW, RIGHT: *Lingerie from the 1996/7 collection*

their standard of living. Due to morning sickness, Janet was often late for work so she brought work home in the evenings. Peter, who had not seen her designs before, was impressed. 'I didn't know you made such pretty things,' he said, and suggested she stay at home with the baby and be a freelance designer. It was the start of Janet Reger!

Still working for Herr Biedermann, she used her summer holiday to complete her first freelance assignment for a swimwear company in Bavaria. It paid a handsome fee, and she worked for them for several years.

Aliza was born on 27 December 1961. Peter advertised Janet's free-lance design service in European news-papers and answered any advertisement he read; work came in quick-ly and soon she was earning four times her previous salary! Soon she had an international clien-tele and travelled reg-ularly round Europe.

In 1966, they had to leave Switzerland and returned to London. In many ways it was another new start: Peter turned sales-man, taking round Janet's sample case and got his first orders at Fenwick's and

joined the Youth for Israel movement and was on her way to live in a kibbutz, Ma'agan Michael, on the Carmel shore. There she met seventeen-year-old Peter Reger, a German. He was thin, had a golden tan, and she was immediately physically attracted to him; he was also arrogant and dictatorial. Within weeks she knew that Peter was the only man for her, but even in those early days there were rows.

After their marriage in January 1961, Peter and Janet worked in Zurich, and, in April, they were shocked to discover Janet was pregnant. Peter's salary was unreliable, and they needed both salaries to maintain

Miss Selfridge. Now they needed to find a way to manufacture the underwear.

A factory in Walthamstow agreed to organize the production. The Regers would buy the cloth and Peter would sell the garments. In June 1967, Janet Reger Creations Ltd was registered and, in August, they made their first deliveries, after some initial difficulties.

Both Janet and Peter realized that this method of working was not ideal and advertised for home workers, but many fell short of Janet's high standards. They then rented a room over a garage in Paddington for £7 a week, installed machinery and gradually built up a small staff. The name of Janet Reger became synonymous with beautiful, sexy underwear. By 1970, they had a staff of twenty.

The materials Janet used were exquisite, including hand-blocked printed chiffon from France and pure silk. With press coverage, orders followed. Soon they realized that direct selling was the way forward; they called their mail-order business Bottom Drawer and it became a little goldmine.

In Southwick Street, they created a workroom and a small basement showroom, then divided the cutting room to make a small, but pretty shop. Bianca Jagger was one of their first customers and others followed – all big spenders.

Their production team was unable to meet the orders and Janet found a tiny factory, formerly a church hall, at St. Mary's Gate in Wirksworth, Derbyshire. From an original staff of about thirty, it grew to 120 in ten years, many of them trained to a high level.

Veronica Holden was an artist employed to paint on silk, who always included a dragonfly in her design and when Janet wanted a logo it had to be a dragonfly. They

also needed a new 'up-market' address and Peter found No 2 Beauchamp Place, a house on three floors plus a basement, in Knightsbridge. Champagne flowed at the opening party – Janet Reger was now a recognized designer of international calibre! Later, Bond Street was targeted, aiming at the super-rich Arabs, and a spacious shop was acquired in nearby Brook Street.

Peter was a person of extreme moods and this was now was starting to have a negative effect on their relationship. The 1970s were golden years for them and many famous people came to their shop. In 1976, Janet visited America, appeared on *Good Morning America*, and returned with huge orders. In 1978, Peter and Janet opened at 12 New Bond Street with a studio at No 103. Sales were excellent, but Peter was concerned at the outgoings; the effects of the oil crisis added to their problems as American trade was devastated by the high pound. Major stores in Britain reduced their orders or no longer stocked Janet Reger garments; instead Janet's styles were copied and mass-produced. Changes had to be made. They started advertising in the *Sunday Times*. The response was excellent and it was money with order. Mail-order sales reached £300,000 in one year.

Sadly, however, within a few years, everything was falling apart: the business was dying, and Janet had decided to leave Peter because of his infidelities. In November 1982, Peter and Janet were advised to go into liquidation but they united to save the business. However, in 1985, Peter Reger committed suicide. Janet still regards him as the only true love of her life and she and Aliza were heartbroken.

Back in business for three years and with things going well, she was conned by a trickster in Dallas, which cost her a lot of money. She was determined to retrieve her trademark, to own her own name, and needed £100,000 which the bank were not willing to lend. She knew that she could get profitable licences if only she owned the trademark. On the day the deal had to be signed, the bank agreed a three-year loan and all was well. Vantona subsequently agreed a good licence for Janet Reger bedlinen.

Thirty years after she started her own business, Janet Reger is still regarded as the finest name in lingerie and nightwear and her production is still diversified between factories and outworkers. Janet's designs, the superb quality of materials and workmanship ensure that Janet Reger creations stand alone. Her early lingerie and nightwear are now collector's pieces.

KANGOL

Jacques Spreiregen was born in Warsaw when it was part of Russia. Later he moved to Britain and became a British citizen. During the First World War he joined the Ambulance Corps, then went to live in France before returning to London. He became a manufacturers' agent, importing Basque berets from France, there being no beret production in Britain at that time. Realizing that an opportunity existed to make them in Britain, he bought a small French firm's manufacturing equipment, hired some of its technicians and started beret production.

met many influential people and was elected a county alderman in 1931. The dole queues in this part of the country were extremely long with unemployment at fifty-four per cent. Thousands were undernourished and there was much social unrest. John Adams was appointed secretary to the Cumberland Development Council and, when the Cumberland Development Company Ltd was formed later, he became its director. In 1949, he became Lord Adams of Ennerdale.

It was through the efforts of John Adams and his links with Whitehall that Jacques Spreiregen and his nephew, Joseph (Jo) Meisner, came to Cleator, near Whitehaven. Together they started to fit out a factory in

John Jackson Adams was born in 1890 in Arlecdon, a little village near Whitehaven, on the edge of the Lake District. He became chairman of the first all-Labour council in England. Through the Independent Labour Party, he

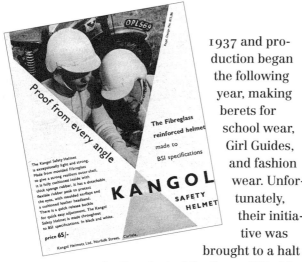

1937 and production began the following year, making berets for school wear, Girl Guides, and fashion wear. Unfortunately, their initiative was brought to a halt by the start of the Second World War – but only temporarily. Before the war, the beret had only been worn by one British Army regiment; now it was selected for general military use and the factory was brought back into full-scale production, making black berets for the Tank Corps; Cyprus blue for the Royal Air Force; maroon for paratroopers – eight different colours in all.

Today, the company still manufactures berets for the British armed forces, and also for many overseas forces.

After the war, the company continued to grow and diversified into different types of men's and ladies' headwear, and, through associated companies, into safety helmets, seat belts and safety harnesses. A second factory was opened in nearby Frizington and this accommodates the knitting plant as well as such processes as dyeing, felting, teasing, shearing and final inspection.

It was Jacques Spreiregen who thought up the name Kangol – derived from the three original raw materials. From silk, he took the K, from angora, he took ANG, and

from wool, he took the OL. KANGOL. Jacques retired from the group in the 1973, and died in 1982. Jo Meisner continued to manage the Headwear Division and his brother, Sylvain Meisner, ran the Safety Division. In 1973, American Safety Equipment bought the company and five years later they were acquired by The Marmon Group, an international association of more than sixty autonomous companies, who are based in Chicago.

New fashion headwear for men, based on the traditional woollen Basque beret, has been developed, including the now famous Kangol 504 Cap. The Kangol Kangaroo was introduced in the 1970s when Kangol headwear became popular with Afro-American males, who would ask for a 'Kanga'. The incumbent president suggested using the stylized kangaroo to further promote the brand. By interchanging styles and colour ranges, the company can produce up to 3,000 different hats at any one time! Kangol has had the Queen's Award to Industry for export achievement.

In the 1980s, Kangol Ltd took over Pickerings of Luton. Luton is the centre of millinery production in the United Kingdom and today Kangol manufactures ladies' fashion and occasion hats there. Another factory in Leeds makes a range of high-class men's hats and the company also makes exclusive hats for celebrities and members of the nobility. Kangol's operations and brand names worldwide were bought out by its management in April 1997.

FACING PAGE, FAR LEFT: *Advertisement in* Vogue, *1953*
FACING PAGE, TOP: *Jacques Spreiregen*
FACING PAGE, BELOW RIGHT: *Mike Tyson*
ABOVE: *Advertisement in* Picture Post, *1955*
ABOVE RIGHT: *Field Marshall Montgomery, wearing a Kangol beret*

LLADRÓ®

Juan, Jose and Vicente Lladró, three brothers, came from a family of market gardeners living in Almacera, then a rural village, now part of the city of Valencia, in Spain.

Juan and Jose enrolled at the local school of arts and crafts, and later Vicente joined them there, where he studied sculpture. Their love was ceramics, but in those early days they had to combine their studies with helping their father in the orchard, or working in a local factory. They were able to put the techniques they had learned into practice when they built a small Moorish-style kiln on the patio of their father's house.

This basic kiln had only a little over fifteen inches of firing space, and it could not reach a high enough temperature to pro-

duce porcelain, but, in the mid-1950s, they used it to start a small manufacturing enterprise. In their small makeshift workshop they carried out their experiments, often toiling through the night after a long day's work. They sold their home-made ceramic flowers to the decorative arts industry, and then began to create classically based pieces similar to those they had seen in European porcelain. However, they admitted that their figures lacked definitive stylistic features.

Once they had started to make sufficient combined income from the sale of their ornaments, they were able to give up their other jobs and start to concentrate fully on

ABOVE: *'Wrestling'*
LEFT: *Juan, Vicente and José Lladró*
FACING PAGE: *'Coiffure'*

the ceramics business. Gradually, the family workshop grew, they employed others to help them and, slowly, the miracle started to occur. Lladró products began to find a place in the market beyond even the wildest dreams of the brothers. What had once been a small part-time business was now turning into a large-scale enterprise. The improved design qualities and expert workmanship of Lladró figures was recognized by collectors and the Lladró family were able to open up new markets which brought added recognition and financial reward.

In the early 1960s, they built a new workshop in neighbouring Tavernes Blanques to accommodate the growing demand for their porcelain figurines. Their first had represented a ballerina on tip-toe; later ones included the 'Sad Harlequin' – both represent elements in the artistic evolution of Lladró. Their artwork is said to be a development from 'classic naturalism', with traditional, academic airs, to 'modern naturalism' which incorporates reminiscences of a sentimental, neo-romantic style with popular overtones – but for the home collector they are seen as items of simple beauty and elegance.

As the company grew, it employed sculptors, chemists, decorators and other specialists and, as a result, new styles and textures were developed. New stoneware figurines, larger and rougher in texture were created. Lladró became available in over eighty countries worldwide. The newly-built workshops at Tavernes Blanques had to be enlarged no less than seven times, two of these extensions taking place within one year, until, in 1969, the foundations were laid for what was to become known as the 'City of Porcelain'.

To ensure its own high standards were maintained the company developed a train-

ing school where its 1,600 employees, mainly women, could learn or develop their skills. Today, everything is still made by hand, preserving the very best traditions, and the company's specialists continue their research and development.

Lladró products are now found in many museums and private collections. In the Bellevue Museum, at the Royal Museums of History and Art in Brussels, outstanding pieces of Lladró porcelain are shown along with porcelain from the eighteenth and nineteenth centuries. Similarly, at the International Museum of Faenza in Italy they have a Lladró sculpture entitled 'Violence'; this is in good company with ceramic work by Picasso, Marc Chagall and Fernand Leger. The Lladró Museum in New York was opened in 1988 on 57th Street, between Fifth and Sixth Avenue. The building contains an auditorium, art gallery and three

LEFT: *'Eighteenth-century Coach'*
BELOW LEFT: *'Valencian Girl'*
BELOW RIGHT: *'Ballerina with Rose'*

FACING PAGE: *Early enamel sign and showcard*

exhibition rooms where visitors can see Lladró's evolution, from the 1950s to the present time, depicted in 1,000 pieces of fine sculpture.

Today Lladró is a world leader in the manufacture of porcelain, and its figurines and other sculpted pieces win the hearts of men and women everywhere.

Alexander McDougall was a shoe merchant in Dumfries in the early 1800s, but later moved to Manchester where he became a schoolmaster, with a special interest in science and mathematics. Finally, in 1845, he set up as a manufacturing chemist, producing such items as sheep dip, scouring soap and disinfectants.

Five of Alexander's sons eventually joined the business and, in 1864, the firm produced a patented substitute for yeast. The McDougall brothers were the first to use the term 'self-raising' flour, and they revolutionized home-baking.

McDougalls first tried to interest bakers in bags of 'phosphatic yeast substitute', but as this did not prove popular, they purchased flour and mixed in the yeast substitute themselves. However, the flour was bought from several different millers and the standards of quality varied. To overcome the problem, the McDougalls became millers themselves, renting premises from Manchester Grammar School.

The business flourished and the McDougall brothers built their own mill in Manchester. Then, in 1869, only five years after they had started in the business, James and John McDougall established a mill in Millwall, London, to enable them to expand their markets in the south of England.

The two milling businesses agreed to divide the country into two parts, drawing a line through Northampton and Birmingham, each undertaking not to sell in the other's zone. The northern section became Arthur McDougall Ltd and the southern one McDougalls Ltd. The two companies re-united in 1926 and McDougalls became a public company in 1933. Sir Robert McDougall, previously chairman of Arthur McDougall, was a great benefactor, giving large tracts of the Peak District to the National Trust and much of the money needed for Manchester University to set up the first large-scale computer.

Towards the end of the 1930s, it became apparent that, if war broke out, the Wheatsheaf Mills, situated in the middle of the London docks, would be vulnerable to air attacks; therefore other mills were acquired in various towns. At Ashton-under-Lyne an immense packaging plant was developed, which was capable of taking over the work of the London mill.

In 1957, Hovis-McDougall Ltd was formed by a merger of the two companies. In 1961, Rank Hovis McDougall Ltd, the biggest group in the milling industry, was created. It is now known as RHM Foods.

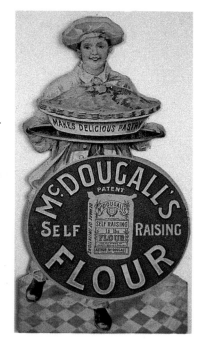

Maxwell House ®

In 1873, when Joel Owsley Cheek reached the age of twenty-one, his father gave him the traditional silver dollar. This represented his freedom to go out into the world to seek his fame and fortune.

Joel left the family farm in Kentucky and joined a firm of wholesale grocers as a travelling salesman, going from village to village. However, it was the coffee that held a special fascination for him and in his spare hours he experimented, selecting different beans, varying their proportions and roasting times – creating new blends.

He spent most of his time searching for the elusive 'perfect blend' of coffee. In 1892, he felt that he had found it. Now he wanted to let the world know, but how could he do this?

He knew that the Maxwell House Hotel in Nashville was where the president, senators, diplomats and leading Europeans met and stayed; could he persuade the management to let him demonstrate *his* blend there? He was sure this would be the best way of testing his judgement. The hotel did co-operate and within weeks distinguished visitors were enjoying his coffee and singing its praises. Many years later, when President Theodore Roosevelt visited the hotel, he was heard to say of the coffee, 'It's good to the last drop.'

Unfortunately, in 1961, the Maxwell House Hotel caught fire and was destroyed. Few people may know of Joel Cheek, but around the world people drink his blend of coffee, thus commemorating the hotel where it first found fame.

Today, Maxwell House coffee is a brand name of Kraft Foods Inc.

ABOVE LEFT: *Joel Cheek*
ABOVE RIGHT: *1923 advertisement*
LEFT: *Maxwell House Hotel*

FACING PAGE, LEFT: *Advertisement in* Needlework, *1946*
FACING PAGE, RIGHT: *Advertisement in* Vogue, *1953*

Newey Goodman Limited

The name of the Newey Group may not be familiar to all, but its products are used by millions every day, particularly women.

The companies include Kirby Beard, which had its beginnings in Gloucester and London in 1743, and J C Newey, founded in Birmingham in the mid-eighteenth century.

William Coucher set up his pin making business in Gloucester, in 1743, and from small beginnings he prospered, established premises in London and became an alderman of that city. In 1803, he took Robert Kirby, a Londoner, into partnership and later George Beard and William Tovey also became partners. The business must have prospered, for in 1816 Robert Kirby was elected a sheriff of London.

Coucher's business took the name Kirby Beard and introduced an automatic pin-making machine from America. Previously pin heads had been fixed manually to their stalks.

Although many pin making businesses failed, Kirby Beard succeeded, particularly in the export trade, possibly because Robert Kirby's nephew, an American, joined the firm.

The company then became Kirby Beard & Kirby. In 1830, it received a Royal Warrant from Queen Adelaide as supplier of pins.

Richard Newey established a small workshop in Birmingham where he made shoe-buckles, whip-mounts and watch-keys and, by the time he died, in 1798, it was a fast expanding business. In Beau Brummel's era, fashions became more complex and there was a need for new accessories and fasteners, tapes and laces no longer being adequate. James Newey was the inventor of the revolutionary 'hook and eye', a product which made the company world-famous, and he also invented the swan-bill hook in 1846.

George Goodman moved to Birmingham from Henley-in-Arden; he bought a patent for making safety pins in 1892.

For these related industries the early years of the twentieth century were good ones, but during the First World War the companies had to concentrate on the war effort. Both Newey and Kirby Beard made hairpins, the latter having produced 450 tons of them in 1914. When hairstyles became shorter, it was necessary to develop a different hairpin; the Kirbygrip has been described as 'a hairpin made of a spring steel that grips the hair and keeps it tidy, while also being practically invisible'. The product was so popular that Kirbygrip became a generic name.

It was the Newey works manager, C B Jerrerd, who developed the snap-fastener (or press-stud), and this was followed, in 1932, by the introduction of the hook-and-eye tape, a boon to ladies as they began to wear brassieres. The slogan, 'If it fastens – Newey's make it!' was becoming justified.

Further innovations came from Goodman's in the 1950s: the 'Snap-Lock' safety pin for fastening babies' nappies, and the 'Easy Cover' button, marketed as 'Trims', which enabled the home dress maker to cover her own buttons with cloth which matched the fabric of the garment.

Newey continued to develop with the

changing times. With the coming of supermarkets, they were the first to introduce blister packs for haberdashery items. Newey products reached so many areas: the pins used in packing shirts or to hold your poppy for Remembrance Day; the safety pin for your dry-cleaning or to hold charity lapel ribbons; the hook-and-eye tape for lingerie and, more recently, poppa fastener tape for fashionable 'teddies' for women. The quantities involved are huge: all the products made in a single year when put end to end would stretch to the moon and back again!

Newey remains a world market leader with its headquarters and main factory, employing 450 workers, in Tipton, West Midlands, a subsidiary manufacturing facility employing 400 in Malaysia and a production unit recently acquired in the Czech Republic.

When Newey absorbed George Goodman it had a total workforce of 2,500. The Newey Group was created in 1975, but in 1978 a twenty-five per cent stake was bought by William Prym-Werke, the largest German manufacturer of hard haberdashery, giving Newey a European dimension.

Today, the company is located in Tipton, not many miles from where Richard Newey made his first products. The present company, with its varied origins, can claim to have greatly influenced how we dress and, particularly, how we fasten our garments.

ABOVE LEFT AND RIGHT: *Early hooks and eyes packaging*
LEFT: *Part of the vast range of Newey products*

FACING PAGE, LEFT: *This book contained over 100 patterns*
FACING PAGE, RIGHT: *Shade cards from which to select knitting yarns*

Patons

By the end of the eighteenth century, hand knitting in Britain was being superseded commercially by machine knitting and this led to a revolution in the textile industry. The main machines involved in this transition were James Hargreaves's Spinning Jenny, Richard Arkwright's spinning and rolling machine, and Samuel Crompton's Mule. Two entrepreneurs who played a large part in this change were James Baldwin, born in 1746, and John Paton, born in 1768.

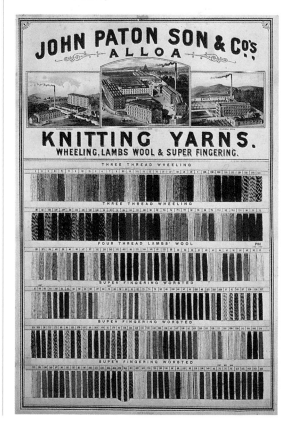

James Baldwin was born in the Yorkshire Pennine town of Halifax and started a wool washing and cloth fulling (cleaning and beating) business there in 1785. James was a strong patriarchal figure, who was referred to as 'Father' by all his family. As the firm expanded, he took one of his sons, John, into partnership and it became J & J Baldwin. Other members of the family later became part of the business which developed into such a major concern that, by the third generation, the family had joined the upper classes. Even in the early days, James Baldwin's home was comfortable, with carpets on the floors, Italian landscapes on the walls, mahogany furniture in the parlour, silver cutlery and a well-stocked cellar.

Book-keeping consisted of a hand-written ledger which also served as a diary where details of family births, marriages and deaths were recorded, as well as major purchases for the home, and even recipes and cures for sicknesses. James's home, water-driven mill and warehouses were all on the same site and some workshops were attached to the house.

In the early days, soaps were bought in from Leeds and Liverpool, whilst whale oil came from Hull; these were used to clean the greasy skins and the yarn. In 1807, Baldwins built a new dye house. Dyes at that time came from natural materials such as lichen and wood, many from overseas sources.

Steam power was introduced to the mill in 1820 and gas lighting in 1826, only four years after it had first come to Halifax.

In 1840, Baldwins was one of the first firms to install Lister's wool combing machine in its mill, although it had to pay Lister £1,000 in royalties. The machine speeded up production and also improved the quality of the finished goods.

James Baldwin was also the company salesman in the early 1800s, and his journeys on horseback took him from Halifax to Preston, Workington, Dumfries, Paisley and Glasgow, returning home by way of Edinburgh, Morpeth, Newcastle, Durham and York. Such expeditions might take six weeks and were not only to bring in sales but also to collect money owed to the firm. When he

died, in 1811, he left £2,957, a considerable sum of money at that time, and a good business to pass down to his children.

It wasn't until 1876 that the famous 'Beehive' device was registered, to protect Baldwins from its competitors.

John Paton's uncle, Andrew Paton, was a dyer in Alloa and John was intrigued by what he saw when he visited the works. Possibly not wanting to compete with his uncle, John chose to produce yarn when he started his own business in about 1811. He bought spinning machinery from England, but soon found that dyeing his own yarn was more profitable. On his father's death, John inherited Kilncraigs House, which he demolished, using the site for a factory extension – this was the origin of Kilncraigs Mill.

Unlike James Baldwin, John Paton lived an austere life and was a temperate man. His employees worked either in the mill or in their own homes, the latter teasing out the raw wool by hand before spinning it on domestic machines. Later, when Hargreaves's Spinning Jenny and Crompton's Mule were brought to Alloa, people came from all around to see the marvellous new machines.

John was eventually joined by his youngest son, Alexander, and the firm became John Paton & Son. When John died in 1848 he left a firm renowned for quality yarns. Their famous 'rose and hand' device, with the motto 'Virtute Viget', which literally means 'it thrives by its goodness', was registered in 1885, followed three years later by the 'white heather and bonnet' device.

Both the Paton and Baldwin families showed great community responsibility, becoming involved in local politics and being benefactors to their own areas. Alexander Paton built a school to provide free education at a time when schooling had to be paid for; on Sundays this was

BEEHIVE KNITTING BOOKLETS No. 17. (New and Enlarged Edition).

Knitted COMFORTS FOR MEN on LAND and SEA

Made from J. J. BALDWINS

'WHITE HEATHER' SPECIALITIES

J. & J. BALDWIN & PARTNERS LTD HALIFAX ENGLAND ESTD. 1785

PRICE TWOPENCE (or by post 2½d.)   All Rights Reserved.

LEFT AND FACING PAGE,
BELOW: *Books of knitting patterns*
RIGHT: *'Virtute viget' means essentially 'it thrives by its goodness'*

used as a Sunday school and for Bible classes. John Baldwin, James's son, said: 'We are sent into the world to be useful to others.'

He lived true to that word as a fine Christian; he became an Honorary Chief Constable of Halifax, the town's first Mayor (with a considerable majority) and, with John Crossley, the carpet manufacturer, founded the *Halifax Courier*.

The Victorian era saw a growth in hand knitting as a hobby as well as a necessity, but, as towns grew larger, fewer women did their own spinning, and more factory-produced knitting yarns became available. In 1896, John Paton, Son & Co Limited produced a book of instructions for knitters, the *Knitting and Crochet Book*, which had 228 pages and over 100 designs for providing clothing for all the family. By the end of the era, thicknesses of yarn had been standardized into two, three and four plys and major spinners were producing pamphlets, the forerunners of today's knitting patterns.

In 1860, the Patons factory burned down, but was rebuilt a year later; by 1872 they employed 450 people. Alexander Forrester, Alexander Paton's brother-in-law, and John Thompson, his nephew, joined the company on John Paton's death, but only after they had changed their names by deed-poll to Alexander Forrester-Paton and John Thompson-Paton. Towards the end of the century, as demand outstripped local wool

supplies, the chairman, John Thompson-Paton, took the entrepreneurial step of sending the company's buyer to Australia to buy wool direct from the producers. The venture was a great success, and in 1906 Patons became a private limited company.

About this time, a number of Yorkshire and Leicestershire companies amalgamated, but the new company, J & J Baldwin & Partners Ltd, was firmly controlled by the Baldwin family.

After the First World War, conditions were ripe for merger. In 1920, Patons and Baldwins Ltd was formed.

Overseas development followed the merger: new factories were opened in Tasmania and China and an existing one was acquired in Canada.

After the Second World War, to accommodate new machinery, the company built new premises on a 140-acre level site the government had designated at Darlington. In the 1960s the company also owned nearly 400 woolshops, many belonging to the Scotch Wool Shop chain.

Unfortunately, production in Halifax has long since ceased and today is centred at the original Kilncraigs Mill in Alloa, whilst the company's head office remains in Darlington.

In 1961, J & P Coats and Patons & Baldwins Limited merged to form the Coats Patons Group, which then merged with Vantona Viyella in 1986 to form the Coats Viyella Group.

PRIMULA®

Olav Kavli was born in 1872 on a farm in the Fannestranden district, on the west coast of Norway, not far from the town of Molde. It was a small farm and life was hard; he saw his mother struggle to make meagre resources go a long way. Even by the age of seven, Olav was determined to rise above the financial hardships of his home and he helped clear stones from a neighbour's fields. The money he earned was put into a bank account in his own name.

One day, on a visit to Molde, with its quay and busy life, he caught a vision of a distant world and, when he was eighteen, he decided to leave home for a new beginning in the city of Bergen. Life there was hard, but Olav had an unsinkable faith in himself and, three years later, he was granted a commercial licence.

At first he just bought and sold cheese, but later he employed a clerk and this

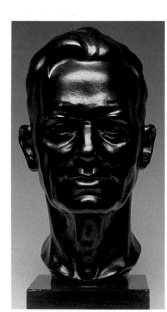

enabled him to expand his trading, first to other parts of Norway, then to America. America was to become one of Kavli's best markets with customers staying loyal to the company for many years. During this formative period he gained a lot of experience and the business prospered.

In 1924, following years of experiment, Olav succeeded in manufacturing a

cheese spread which had long-life qualities and was to be the start of a new chapter in his life. The growth of sales of Primula cheese was phenomenal and Knut Kavli, Olav's son and now also his partner, quickly realized that any further growth would have to involve establishing companies in other countries. During the 1930s, production units were established in Austria, Denmark and Sweden. Kavli started manufacturing cheese

spread in the United Kingdom in 1936 and moved to a new factory in Gateshead, Tyne & Wear in 1957. In their modern factory, the company now makes 4,000 tons of Primula cheese spread products each year.

One of the marketing successes of Primula cheese spread has been the distinctive half-moon shaped wooden boxes. They were first made for Kavli in a small workshop outside Bergen where the top and bottom halves were punched out and the sides were stapled by hand. In those early days the label, depicting the well-known 'Primula girl' was stuck on by hand, twenty girls completing 6,000 boxes a day.

But who was the Primula girl? She was a piece of Olav Kavli's fantasy, created for public relations purposes! The concept was of a dairymaid in Norwegian national costume, set in a Norwegian landscape. The original drawing was the work of a German

10 million tubes of Primula cheese spread in a variety of flavours are sold in the United Kingdom alone.

What is cheese spread? It is made by taking high quality cheese and replacing the cheese protein's calcium ions with sodium ions from sodium phosphate; this makes the cheese water soluble and amenable to heat treatment.

In addition to Primula cheese spread, Kavli have introduced a long-life, fresh-tasting dip, a range of sandwich fillers and a ninety-five per cent fat-free cheese spread with extra vitamins and minerals.

On the death of Knut Kavli in 1962, ownership was transferred to a charitable trust, which supports cultural research and humanitarian projects, and which removes the risk of takeover.

FACING PAGE, LEFT: *Bust of Olav Kavli*
FACING PAGE, RIGHT: *Advertisement in* Punch, *1956*
LEFT: *The Primula Girl*
BELOW: *Modern packs of Primula in a variety of containers*

artist in the 1950s, and this was later re-designed in the United States. The primula, or primrose, is the first flower of spring and the young girl epitomizes this. Over the years, although her basic features have stayed the same, she has changed with the fashions of the times. Many varieties of Primula cheese spread have been introduced, the earliest being 'Primula with Alpine Spices' in 1929, the same year that Primula also became available in tubes. Today, some

Procter&Gamble

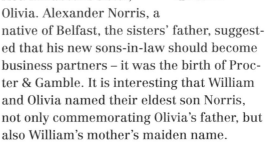

The Reverend Henry Procter was vicar at Orleton, about twenty-five miles from Worcester, from 1733 to 1767. He was succeeded by his son, the Reverend Thomas Procter, from 1767 to 1815. Between them they had twenty children! The last but one of Thomas's children, William, married Sarah Cooper and they named their first-born son William after his father.

This lad grew to be a man of great courage, with initiative, independence and a thirst for adventure. A younger brother had emigrated to America and William and his wife Martha followed. They landed at Baltimore in 1821, and then moved to Wheeling at the head of the Ohio River. There, along with a fellow countryman, William built a flat-boat and sailed down river to Cincinnati. Here, however, Martha was taken gravely ill with cholera and died.

William, filled with grief, was a stranger in an unknown land; he decided to stay in the town and found work in a bank. Not enjoying this, and finding there was a need for good quality candles in the area, he started making them in his spare time. On his regular visits to market to sell the candles he met a quiet, gentle-natured man, James Gamble.

James's family came from Enniskillen, but had decided to make a new start in America. He was sixteen when he arrived in Cincinnati with his parents and their other children. Two years later, he was apprenticed to a soap and candle maker and, in 1828, he started his own business.

In 1833, James Gamble married Elizabeth Norris in Cincinnati and, later the same year, William Procter married Elizabeth's sister, Olivia. Alexander Norris, a native of Belfast, the sisters' father, suggested that his new sons-in-law should become business partners – it was the birth of Procter & Gamble. It is interesting that William and Olivia named their eldest son Norris, not only commemorating Olivia's father, but also William's mother's maiden name.

It was a difficult time to start a business: there was concern that the United States was bankrupt, and many banks were closing down. Cincinnati had fourteen other soap and candle makers, but Procter & Gamble had a calmness which carried them through adversity. They took as their sign, an unofficial trademark, 'The Moon and Stars'. Although there was rumour of civil war in the 1850s, they pressed ahead and built a new plant to allow their business to expand. When the war came, they won orders to supply the Union armies. They established their own research laboratory, one of the first in America, and by 1890 they controlled a

multi-million dollar corporation which sold more than thirty types of soap.

In 1879, James Norris Gamble, a son of the founder and a trained chemist, developed a high quality, inexpensive white soap. Its name, 'Ivory', came to Harley Procter, son of the other founder, as he read in Psalm 45: 'out of ivory palaces'. Their soap had purity, mildness and was long-lasting.

Production began at their new Ivorydale factory, which incorporated a pleasant work environment – a progressive approach at that time. Soon, the company introduced Ivory Flakes for washing clothes and dishes. In 1896, Procter & Gamble, now an incorporated company, issued their first colour print advertisement in the *Cosmopolitan* magazine, picturing the Ivory Lady.

In 1911, the company introduced 'Crisco', an all-vegetable shortening, providing a healthier substitute for animal fats, and built its first manufacturing plant in Ontario, Canada, to produce it and the Ivory soap. The company, having the interests of its workers at heart, in 1919 revised its articles of incorporation to include that the 'interests of the Company and its employees are inseparable'.

As electric light became popular, the trade in candles declined and, in the 1920s, Procter & Gamble ceased production of them. The popular Camay perfumed beauty soap was introduced in 1926 and Oxydol and Dreft appeared in the early 1930s. William Cooper Procter, the last member of the founding families to control the company, died in 1934.

In 1930, in a bid to develop overseas trade, Procter & Gamble purchased Thomas Hedley & Co Ltd of Newcastle upon Tyne. Hedley had also begun his soap making business in 1837, its principal product being Fairy household soap, a very popular brand in the north of England.

When television was introduced in the United States in 1939, Procter & Gamble was one of its first advertisers. In 1943, it created a drug division to promote its growing range of toiletries.

Early post-war products included Tide, which was described as the 'New Washing Miracle', and Crest, the first fluoride toothpaste, which, in 1960, the American Dental Association recognized as 'an effective decay-preventative dentifrice'.

In 1934, using 1810-style packaging and a 1781 logo, William Lightfoot Schultz started selling 'Early American Old Spice'. In 1957, Old Spice, now a Procter & Gamble product, was introduced into the United Kingdom, one of the earliest of men's toiletries, stressing the importance of 'masculine freshness'.

Other well-known companies which have become part of the empire include Max Factor, Shulton and Vick's. In 1992 the Max Factor company was renamed Procter & Gamble. P & G is now a multinational company embracing a wide range of household and luxury products, many of them in daily use in homes worldwide. Company sales now exceed $30 billion a year, over half of which are from sales outside the United States.

FACING PAGE, TOP LEFT: *William Procter*
FACING PAGE, TOP RIGHT: *1882 advertisement for Ivory soap*
FACING PAGE, BELOW RIGHT: *James Gamble*
ABOVE: *Enamel sign for Fairy soap*

Samuel Smith was born in a cottage in Lady Pit Lane, Leeds in 1872 and was already helping to support the family when he was only nine, working as a butcher's boy on Friday nights and Saturdays.

At the age of ten he went to work in the tea trade as a half-timer, impressing his employers with his enthusiasm and capacity for hard work. He started as an errand boy. However, although he had had little formal education, he was bright and cheerful and was an obvious choice to become a sales-man, later becoming one of the company's most outstanding. By the time he was thirty-five, he held a senior position in the compa-ny he had served loyally for twenty-five years, and knew as much about the tea trade as anyone in the country.

The first door-to-door van delivery sys-

tem was introduced to Sheffield shortly before the turn of the century. This method of selling tea gripped Sam's imagination. In 1907, to the surprise of his employers and friends, he gave up his job and left the Leeds area, not wanting to be in competition with his employers. In Newcastle upon Tyne he formed a partnership with William Tittering-ton, and Sam devised the name 'Ringtons' from the last seven letters of his name. The firm's first premises were a rented lock-up shop in Third Avenue, Newcastle; Sam had £250 capital and his first purchases were a horse, a van, utensils and a stock of tea.

The partners had to stimulate a demand for their tea. Local housewives were suspi-cious, but Sam's 'Yorkshire grit', hard work and knowledge of the tea trade won them over; he was also selling his fine blend teas at competitive prices. A year later, he acquired two horse-drawn vans, took on four assistants, and the firm moved to larg-er premises in an abandoned rifle range in Shields Road. The Ringtons' vans, with their distinctive lettering and colours became a familiar sight on the streets of Tyneside, and the friendly sales-teams, with regular deliv-eries of high quality teas, won hundreds of new customers.

The First World War was a devastating blow for Ringtons; by now it had eleven vans, seventeen assistants, and a flourishing

FACING PAGE, TOP: *Sam Smith with his wife*
FACING PAGE, BELOW: *William Titterington*
LEFT: *Advertisement from 1953*
RIGHT: *Advertisement from 1939*
BELOW: *The last horse-drawn delivery van*

business. Fifteen of the men were conscripted, but Sam promised to keep their jobs open until the end of the war, and help their families in whatever way he could. Not only did he lose his staff, but rationing and other restrictions put his sales in jeopardy. Grocers told customers that if they wanted to buy sugar they must also buy the grocer's tea – this put his business at even greater risk and Ringtons' tea sales dropped dramatically. In a desperate effort to survive, he sold dried eggs, tinned and evaporated milk, canned meat, pickles and a variety of other products. Prices were regulated, sometimes at a level lower than Ringtons could buy at.

After the war, there was little business left, but, true to his word, Sam re-engaged the twelve staff who had survived and set about rebuilding it. Housewives flocked to the Ringtons' vans to buy quality tea, something they had missed during the war.

In 1926, Ringtons opened a new head office and factory in Algernon Road, Newcastle. Soon it recruited more new staff and opened depots all over the north of England. The early premium offers are collectors' items today. In 1927, Sam had a special satisfaction when he opened a depot in Leeds

and again, in 1935, when Ringtons opened a blending and packing plant on the site of the cottage where he had been born sixty-three years before. Later Ringtons introduced motor-vans, but housewives preferred the horse-drawn vehicles. Mechanization was not completed until 1954.

Sam Smith died in 1949, but he had trained other members of the family in the intricacies of the tea trade, and they took responsibility for the company.

Over the years, Ringtons has diversified and met the challenge of change, one diversification being to set up its own coach-building section. Other companies came to it for vehicles and a subsidiary, Northern Coachbuilders, was formed. Today it trades as Smith's Electric Vehicles in Gateshead's Team Valley.

The current managing director of Ringtons is Nigel Smith, Sam's great-grandson.

Royal Doulton

John Doulton was born in Fulham, London, in 1793. When only twelve years old he was apprenticed at the Fulham Pottery, which had been founded in the seventeenth century by John Dwight, often regarded as the father of English ceramics. It was an excellent training ground for the young lad.

In 1812, having completed his apprenticeship, he worked at the Vauxhall Walk pottery, one of many in that part of London. It was owned by Martha Jones, widow of the previous owner. She had intended to hand it on to her son, Edward, but he got into trouble with the law, fled on a ship to South America, and nothing was heard of him for the next thirty years. Martha asked her foreman, John Watts, to find someone to replace Edward and he recommended Doulton.

John Doulton worked hard and was soon able to do any work which was asked of him, from preparing the clay to firing the kilns. In 1815, Martha Jones, not having heard of her son for three years, took Watts and Doulton into partnership and the firm became Jones, Watts and Doulton. There was intense competition from other potteries in the area and some days John Doulton worked at the potter's wheel from six o'clock in the morning until late into the evening; on other days he went to seek orders or collect payments before working at the wheel. The clay was broken with hammers and trodden by foot, but later the partners rented some adjoining land and set up a grinding and mixing mill which was powered by a blind horse.

The bulk of the work was the making of plain stoneware bottles and jugs, but they also produced finely-modelled brown mugs and jugs in the likeness of Nelson, Wellington and Napoleon, spirit flasks in the shape of pistols and powder horns, and hunting jugs and mugs with reliefs of horsemen and hounds, and stags and foxes. Other items included candlesticks, inkstands and tobacco jars.

In 1820, Mrs Jones withdrew from the partnership which became Watts and Doulton, although later better known as Doulton and Watts. As the business grew, larger premises in Lambeth High Street allowed

FACING PAGE, TOP: *John Doulton 1793–1873*
FACING PAGE, BELOW: *Former Doulton factory on the Albert Embankment, c. 1885*
LEFT: *Salt-glazed stoneware figure tankard depicting Lord Nelson, c. 1821–30*
BELOW: *Advertisement in* Punch, *1953*

future extensions to the factory. The passing of the Reform Act in 1832 gave rise to the production of many thousands of stoneware 'Reform Bottles' and 'Reform Flasks', depicting the heads and shoulders of William IV and Lords Grey, Brougham and Russell, who had been closely associated with the Bill.

Henry Doulton, John's second son, entered the business in 1835, keen to become a practical potter. He worked hard in the pottery during the day, and in the evenings he studied perspective drawing, metallurgy, chemistry and physics, as well as pursuing his love of history and literature. Within two years, he was making 20-gallon vessels on the potter's wheel. It was Henry who devised how the potter's wheel could be driven by steam. In 1841, to celebrate his coming of age, he made a 300-gallon 'Ali Baba' chemical transport jar, which was proudly displayed as the largest stoneware vessel in the world.

Sculptures and architectural terracotta, decorative chimney pots and garden ornaments were now featured in the growing list of products. In 1846, Henry established the first factory in the world for the production of stoneware drainpipes and related wares and soon miles of them were being laid below the streets of towns and cities. Further additions included kitchen sinks, wash basins and sanitary ware. Following the

company's exhibit at the 1871 First International Exhibition in London, Queen Victoria took a keen interest in the achievement of the Doulton artists. During the 1860s, John Sparkes, principal of the Lambeth School of Art, persuaded the now famous potter to branch out into art. The pottery was a perfect mix of industry and artistic expression and won the Grand Prix at the Paris Exhibition of 1878; the salt-glazed stoneware achieved international acclaim.

In 1877, Henry Doulton and his brother James acquired a major holding in Pinder, Bourne & Co of Burslem, in the Staffordshire Potteries. Here the Doultons entered the field of fine earthenware and the company became Doulton & Co, Burslem in 1882, on the retirement of Shadford Pinder. As at Lambeth, Doulton brought together a fine team of designers, modellers and artists to create bone-china table centre-pieces, vases

A time to reflect on **THE VALUE OF TRADITION**

During the Coronation ceremonies crown and coronet, velvet and ermine, tabard and tunic, cockade and crested plume create a spectacle to excite the imagination. And tradition, that golden thread linking past achievement with present inspiration, fills our minds.

Not least of Britain's traditions is that of making fine pottery for the home. The first Doulton pottery, established in Lambeth in 1815, linked up with centuries of local ceramic activity and—through the delftware and stoneware potters—with yet older traditions reaching back to the ancient East. During the past 138 years the House of

Doulton has added several glorious chapters to the story of British pottery making. In 1887, Henry Doulton was knighted by Queen Victoria for his services to the industry and, in 1901, King Edward VII conferred on the Company the rarely bestowed right to use the word "Royal" in describing its products. Today, in the reign of our new Queen, Elizabeth II, Royal Doulton craftsmen are maintaining the Company's highest traditions. The work of their hands—including tableware in bone china and fine earthenware, Royal Doulton figures, animal models, Toby and character jugs, and decorated stoneware ceramics —is eagerly sought the world over.

ROYAL DOULTON

DOULTON & CO. LIMITED, DOULTON HOUSE, ALBERT EMBANKMENT, LONDON, S.E.1

and plates of exquisite beauty. In 1884, a new wing was built for the manufacture of fine bone china and another talented team was recruited to produce bone-china tableware and tea-sets for export to America and Australasia.

Accolades continued to come to Henry Doulton, including a knighthood in 1887. Doulton took 1,500 items of ceramics to the Chicago Exhibition in 1893 – something no other pottery in the world could match – and won seven of the highest awards. Henry died in 1897, aged seventy-seven. His had

been a life of dedication, energy and great fulfilment.

After his death, a limited company was formed, directed by his son Henry Lewis Doulton, and after him by Sir Henry's only grandson, Eric Hooper. In 1901, Edward VII conferred a rare honour on the company by not only presenting its chairman with the Royal Warrant but also specifically authorizing the use of the word 'Royal' to describe its products.

In more recent years, Royal Doulton has become known for its English translucent china, now English Fine China, which is used in homes throughout the world. Its designs for children have also become great favourites, particularly the Bunnykins range introduced in 1934. Collectors find interest in all areas of Doulton and Royal Doulton productions, but are particularly catered for by a wide range of commemorative wares. Today, the company includes such well-known names as Royal Crown Derby, Minton and Royal Albert. Royal Doulton now has an annual turnover of over £230 million.

TOP LEFT: *'The Dante Vase', with scenes from Dante's* Inferno, *1893*
LEFT: *Advertisement from* Pottery Gazette, *1934, showing the Gaylee tableware design*
TOP RIGHT: *A selection of subjects representing more than fifty years of Royal Doulton figure production*

Scott's Porage Oats

In the time of Robbie Burns, many Scottish peasants and agricultural workers relied on potatoes, milk, vegetables and Scotch oatmeal, in the form of porridge and oat cakes, for sustenance. Indeed, 'the use of oatmeal porridge as a breakfast, and oatmeal cakes or whole wheatmeal bread in the course of the day was essential to the healthy, vigorous development of the young of both sexes in a Scotch climate'. It was at a much later date that bread made from fine white wheaten flour came into use.

A & R Scott, two brothers, started making Scott's Midlothian Oat Flour in 1880, in the Kingston Dock area of Glasgow. Little appears to be known of the brothers, the business being run from an early date by partners Robert Lauder, who looked after the technical aspects, and William Allen, who controlled the finances.

Quite quickly Scott's Midlothian Oat Flour was becoming well known in the area, for, in 1884, an industrial periodical *The Mercantile Age* was reporting on the high quality of both the product and the methods used at Scott's mill: on the fourth floor, which had a floor area of 13,000 square feet, was the 'most ingenious milling machinery that we have ever seen'. The oats came to the mill as groats and then the hull, or husks, and the germs were removed. The germ was regarded as a deleterious substance, interfering with the digestibility of the oat flour. Other oatmeals generally caused irritation of the stomach or bowels. After the oat flour had been thoroughly purified, it travelled

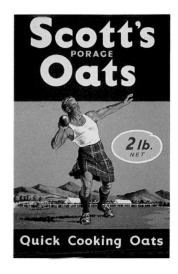

down a chute and was emptied on to zinc tables 25-feet long by 5-feet wide. Girls then put the oat flour into tins or canisters, varying in size from ½lb to 10lbs. At that time 1,000 1lb-tins were packed each day, as well as the other sizes. The ground floor was the bakery where the oat cakes and biscuits were prepared and 'fired'. The second and third floors were offices and packing rooms.

The mill was always scrupulously cleaned and, even in 1884, everything was done by automatic machinery, the flour not being touched even by the packers' hands. The girls hermetically sealed the canisters, labelled and packed them. Each girl bore enviable marks of health and happiness and an air of comfort pervaded the floor. Exporting was already taking place to the West

ABOVE: *The famous Scott's 'Porage' Oats package, c. 1950*
BELOW: *Biscuit packaging from the 1880s*

Indies, New Zealand, America and all parts of the Continent. The oat flour was recommended for infants only a few weeks old and equally for invalids and adults.

The firm was already also making Scott's Midlothian Biscuits in 1884, and in 1893, in *The Victualling Trades Review*, it was stated that 'Scott's Oatcakes and Oat-flour Biscuits are universally appreciated, while at home they form a prominent feature at the tables of the richest and humblest in the land'. Once a fortnight there was a regular order from the Prince of Wales! Now, Scott's had premises in Buchan Street and was sending out from its 'model bakery' 32,000 oat cakes each week.

By 1888, the firm had become a limited

company and, in 1909, larger premises were acquired at West Mills, Colinton, Edinburgh.

To distinguish Scott's Oat Flakes from their competitors, the description Scott's Porage Oats was introduced in 1914 and remains a trademark to the present day. The word 'Porage' is a mixture of the old Scottish word 'Poray' and the French word 'Potage'. In 1924, the well-known symbol of the Highlander Putting the Shot was added to the packaging. It is suggested that the figure was modelled on an NCO in the King's Own Scottish Borderers, whose barracks were not far from Colinton Mills.

A disastrous fire destroyed much of the production area in 1928, but with help from the dedicated workforce the mill was up and running again within seven weeks. In 1947, a former flax mill was acquired at Cupar, Fife, to manufacture Scott's Porage Oats. A & R Scott Ltd was taken over by Cerebos Ltd in 1955, and both were acquired by Rank Hovis McDougall in 1969. In 1982, A & R Scott was bought by Quaker Oats Ltd, one of their main competitors, and, from 1989, Cupar became the main centre of Quaker's milling operation in Europe, the expanded mill being the largest oatmill in Western Europe.

ABOVE LEFT: *Packaging products in factory, 1926*
ABOVE RIGHT: *Advertisement from 1957*
LEFT: *Advertisement in* John Bull, *1954*

FACING PAGE: *An early advertisement featuring the 'Tom-Tom' man*

Sharwood's

When James Allen Sharwood went to work as a foreign correspondent for a London insurance company, he followed a family tradition, although unfortunately his father had become bankrupt. Now, James was starting on the ladder to success, but knew the risk of failure.

He already had a sound knowledge of three European languages, for he had had a good education which included two years in Heidelberg. His mother was of Scottish extraction and her motto was 'Be thorough' – which he took to heart.

Within a fortnight of joining the insurance company, he discovered that the highest jobs were those of the actuaries. In a year, he had become an insurance agent, aware of the value of life insurance and selling these policies to others.

Fate took a hand, however, for, when an uncle died, his widow invited James to help with running his business. Now he had to study another area – the wine trade. His life abroad and intimate knowledge of French, Spanish and German helped him, and he diligently read what few books he could find on the subject. He also became personally involved in all aspects of the trade – blending of spirits, bottling, studying vintages, etc. Here, as in the world of insurance, his guiding principle was 'Be thorough'. Two or three years later, he was invited to open a wine and spirit department by an old-established grocery company and, in about three years, had built up trade to £20,000 a year, a considerable sum at that time. A little later, when the head of the firm died, he became a

controlling partner of the whole business. Over the next three or four years, he devoted thirteen or fourteen hours a day to developing a business that had been rather antiquated, and this gave him the opportunity to become thoroughly acquainted with the distributive side of the grocery trade.

James was asked by a family friend of the Viceroy of India, Lord Dufferin, if he could supply and ship continental conserves and other foods, which they were finding difficult to obtain, to the Viceroy's French chef in India. Few shops stocked such delicacies and James Sharwood had no experience of these commodities, but his enterprising spirit and his knowledge of French and the Continent enabled him to fulfil the request. Repeat orders soon followed. The trade brought him into contact with foreign manufacturers and was to be instrumental in him founding his own business.

In 1889, at 77 Carter Lane, in the City of London, he opened as an importer and

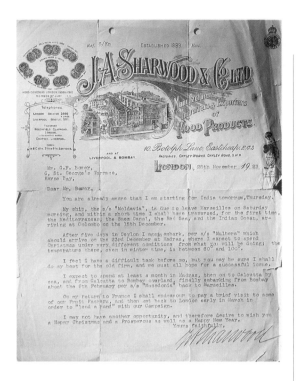

exporter of foreign produce. It was a venture of faith, for he had little capital, little experience in that field and few connections, but he had self-confidence and an ability to recognize an opportunity when it occurred. His rented premises were modest, comprising a small office, double basement and a sale room above. He worked all hours of the day and frequently made long night journeys to build up the business, but, whatever the stress of time, he freely admitted that he was never tempted to work on a Sunday, and that his affairs never suffered as a consequence.

In 1896, James settled with his father's creditors and was able to secure the annulment of his father's bankruptcy.

Around 1890, James was dealing in a French product, tinned peas, at that time only produced on the Continent. Due to a severe drought at the critical period, the crop of *petits pois* was a failure, so he bought half a million tins from Holland – that year Sharwood's was almost the only company able to supply that delicacy.

On another occasion, a strange, foreign-looking figure, a Frenchman, called at the office in Carter Lane. He couldn't speak any English, but when he discovered that James Sharwood could speak French, he was able to offer him crystallized and glacé fruits on behalf of one of the oldest French producers. Feeling at home, he poured out his story and got an order . . . and James Sharwood saw the start of an import and export business in which he would become a world expert. For thirty years, he spent many weeks each year in Provence among the producers and manufacturers, learning about packing and marketing. He encouraged new packaging of mixed fruits, which were suitable for presents, and also new glacé and crystallized fruits such as apricots, greengages, figs, pink and white pears, cherries and oranges. Later, crystallized violets, rose petals, mimosa and other flowers, preserved in sugar, were brought over from the South of France, largely introduced by James. Another of his guiding principles was: 'Make it easy for the grocer to show and sell the goods, and for the customer to buy them.' He also popularized the sale of shiny silver balls, *boules argentées*, of various sizes, which can transform an iced cake.

At that time, to many people, chutney was merely a name, often only bought by Anglo-Indians who had learnt to appreciate it in the East. It is fair to say that it was James Sharwood who made chutney a household word. In the City was a small importing house which bought flavouring essences from Sharwood's. The owners ran up a bill and couldn't pay and the proprietor suggested that Mr Sharwood might take some 'Ship Brand' chutney instead. James did so, but it sat on his shelves for twelve months before he persuaded one of his travellers to introduce it to his customers. At once, it was such a success that the stock was soon exhausted and he had to send to Bombay, to Manockjee, Poonjiajee & Sons, the makers, for a further consignment. This was the beginning of a growing stream of chutney flowing into Britain. When the sterling value of the rupee was low, Sharwood was able to supply chutney to grocers cheaply, so they could sell it at a price popular with the public.

James Sharwood was a good salesman and he travelled to see grocers, who often said, 'Send me a dozen.' His reply was, 'No! I would rather not. If you have *only* a dozen you will put it on your shelves and there it will remain. Let me send you at least a case of six dozen. You can then show it in your window and it will sell like hot cakes.' His recommendations were justified by sales.

FACING PAGE: *A letter from James Sharwood on the eve of his trip to India, November 1923*
ABOVE, RIGHT: *Curry powder was one of the products brought back from India in 1924*
BELOW: *Chinese sauces are an important part of today's business*

After the First World War, Sharwood's introduced 'Green Label' and supported it with an extensive advertising campaign, adopting the 'Tom-Tom' man as its trademark.

In 1923/4 James visited India to discuss chutney business, but he also bought curry powder and other condiments. Manockjee, Poonjiajee & Sons became an integral part of Sharwood's, and Vencatachellum, producers of curry powder, also came under Sharwood's control. From France he brought in olive oil. James Sharwood fought and won a famous lawsuit for the right to use the term 'tomato ketchup', against an American firm who wanted monopoly of the name – something all makers of tomato ketchup should be grateful for.

In the early 1960s, the company was acquired by Rank Hovis McDougall and now forms part of RHM Grocery Ltd.

Today, Sharwood's is the main supplier of Indian and Chinese food to the major supermarkets and other multiples. It also imports substantial quantities of tomato purée from Italy's Po Valley. The company is still innovative, as demonstrated by the production of 'Ready-to-Eat Puppodums' and many authentic Indian and Chinese sauces.

SHIPPAMS

In 1786, Charles Shippam opened for business as a grocer in Chichester's Westgate. As the business grew so did his family – he had ten children, four of them boys. George, the third son, later started his own tea and grocery business in North Street, but it was his son, another Charles, who was to play a major part in the development of Shippams.

Charles leased 48 East Street (still part of Shippams) to trade as a pork butcher. In the early days he was described as 'Pork Butcher and Bacon Curer and Maker of the Celebrated Chichester Sausages', selling 'Fine Home Cured and York Hams' and 'Home Cured and Wiltshire and Gloucester Bacon'. The famous Chichester sausages were first made in 1855 and only discontinued in 1970.

Next door was Fred Cooper's grocer's shop. Charles married Fred's niece, Caroline, and they had eleven children. When Fred

retired in 1889, Charles took over his lease and in 1894 bought the freehold. He had already bought other sites and now he used the premises at East Street for production purposes and for accommodating staff.

The growth of the railways in the second half of the nineteenth century meant that local traders, like Charles Shippam, could now transport their goods quickly over a wide area of the country and gave enterprising businessmen the opportunity to serve a much larger market. Charles took advantage of this to supply his sausages to towns along the south coast and the southern London suburbs, and in 1894 he appointed his first sales representative.

Behind the shop, in 1886, Charles started packing his products in cans to supply the armed forces. Initially, it was sausages, but soon the range was extended to include canned galantines (cooked cold meat in jelly), pies, pâtés, potted meats, whole pheasant, whole chicken, ox tongues and soup. Later, he also supplied products in glass jars, and, in 1894, Shippams introduced a range of potted meats and fish pastes packed in earthenware pots. The contents of these pots were sealed by pouring liquid butter onto the surface of the paste and allowing it to set. Many of the early recipes have survived and, with small alterations to conform to modern legislation, are still popular on the tea tables of homes throughout the country.

When Charles died in 1897 he left everything to his wife, Caroline, but in 1899 five of their eight sons formed a partnership and in 1913 this became a private limited company.

In the early years of the twentieth century, glass jars became available which could be heat processed to allow the contents to be sterilized, and thereby given an indefinite shelf life. This was particularly important when shops and homes had no refrigerators and, by 1910, the glass jars had replaced the earthenware containers for potted meats and pastes.

During the first half of this century, Shippams continued to manufacture and market canned and bottled products, many being based on chicken meat. It was therefore natural that, in 1960, the company should introduce a range of chicken products, complete with various sauces. Today Shippams is the largest canner of chicken in the United Kingdom, supplying not only products under its own name, but also 'own brand' products for companies such as Marks & Spencer, Sainsbury's and Tesco.

Shippams remained a family business until 1975, when it became a wholly owned subsidiary of William Underwood Company of Boston, Massachusetts. In 1982, Underwood's was acquired by IC Industries, now called the Whitman Corporation. Their products include such famous names as 'Old El Paso' Mexican foods, 'Progresso' soups and Italian foods, 'Sweet 'N' Low' diet foods and sugar substitutes, as well as products manufactured in Sweden, Australia, Venezuela, Canada and the United States. The Corporation not only has the world's largest Pepsi-Cola bottling franchise but, through the Hussman Corporation, it is the world's leading producer of refrigeration systems, and, through Midas International, has the world's leading franchised motor car servicing operation.

In February 1995, the company was acquired by Grand Metropolitan plc and so, after twenty years of American ownership, Shippams was now back in British hands. Unfortunately, GrandMet decided, in June 1996, to sell off their national brands and thus, at the time of writing, Shippams is back on the market.

Back at Shippams, John Shippam, Charles's great-great-great-grandson is Personnel Manager. Shippams are proud of their long tradition of supplying fine meat and fish products, but particularly pastes. They still seek to excite the tastebuds!

FACING PAGE ABOVE: *Early advertisement*
FACING PAGE BELOW: *Grocers Exhibition, Earls Court, c. 1910*
RIGHT *The Chichester factory, 1958*

SONY®

Akio Morita was born in 1921, the fifteenth-generation heir to one of Japan's finest and oldest sake-brewing families. His father asked a venerable Japanese scholar of Chinese lore and literature for advice as to what name he should call his son. He recommended the name Akio (pronounced Aki), which uses the character for 'enlightened'; this, when coupled with Morita, which means 'prosperous rice-field', gave a name which pleased his parents.

When Akio was about ten or eleven years old, he was taken by his father to see how the family business was run, even sitting through long board meetings. He was taught to talk to the workers, being reminded, 'You are the boss from the start. You are the eldest son in the family. Remember that.' Whilst he was given full awareness of his future privileges and responsibilities, he was also taught that he should not dominate people, nor use them as scapegoats. He was also encouraged to embrace the philosophy that you use the motivations you share with

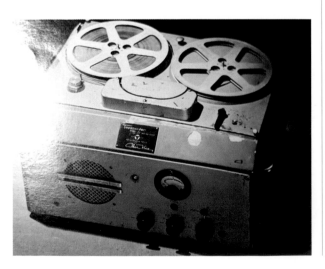

people to accomplish something that will be of advantage to both of you. Already he was developing a management philosophy that was to stay with him throughout his business life – that a manager needs to cultivate patience and understanding, to avoid selfishness and meanness.

Akio's family was to some degree westernized: his father went to work in a chauffeur-driven Buick car, whilst at home the family had a General Electric washing machine and a Westinghouse refrigerator. Akio's father had spent 600 yen on one of the first phonographs (when a Japanese car cost about 1,500 yen), so anxious was he to have the best reproduction of music. Listening to their first record, Ravel's 'Bolero', the young Akio was determined to build his own electric phonograph and record his own voice.

When Akio was in middle school, he heard about a German steel-belt recorder which the Japanese Broadcasting Company

an interdisciplinary team trying to perfect thermal-guidance weapons and night vision gunsights, but time had run out. They did not realize the horror of the occasion, having been told that the bomb was a new kind of weapon that flashed and shone. After the second atomic bomb, on Nagasaki, Emperor Hirohito made a radio announcement on 15 August 1945, saying the war was over. He told the nation the future would be grim and said they must devote their strength to the construction of the future, challenging them to keep pace with the progress of the world.

Akio started to work with Masaru Ibuka, a brilliant engineer whom he had met during the war. In an old empty building they discussed what business they might run – they had the concept of being innovators, making new high-technology products in ingenious ways.

Through the perseverance of a friend they were asked to make a large broadcast mixing unit for NHK Broadcasting Company. When they were delivering the unit, Ibuka

had imported; about the same time Dr Kenzo Nagai had produced a wire-recorder. Akio spent about a year trying to make a similar recorder using piano wire but, although unsuccessful, he was not discouraged, having by now developed a great love of physics.

In 1940, with Japan on the brink of war with the United States, Akio made preparations to go to Osaka Imperial University to study applied physics. His father was disappointed that he did not choose economics, but did not try to change his mind. Eventually, Akio took a commission in the Navy which allowed him to complete his studies and do further research work. On 6 August 1945, Akio was having lunch with naval colleagues when news came through of the atomic bomb on Hiroshima. He was part of

FACING PAGE, ABOVE: *Akio Morita*
FACING PAGE, BELOW: *Early reel-to-reel tape recorder*
ABOVE AND RIGHT: *Sony Walkman, 1979*

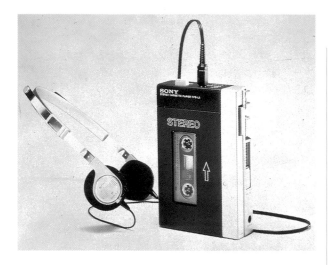

noticed an American tape recorder, the first he had ever seen. Reluctantly, the company allowed him to take the recorder back to show Akio and both agreed that this was the project for them.

Their first problem was how to make the tape; they had no plastic so they tried cutting inadequate cellophane into ¼-inch wide strips and covering it with various experimental coatings, but it stretched and was useless. Next they tried good-quality kraft paper, cutting it with razor blades. The long strips again had to be coated, and, as they had no electric furnace, the oxalic ferrite was heated in a frying pan, the hot material being painted on by hand.

Unfortunately, the public did not share their enthusiasm for tape recorders. They had to accept that the machine had to be 'sold' to an indifferent public; they had to discover a market for the invention. In Japanese courts, there was a shortage of stenographers; they demonstrated their machine to the Japan Supreme Court and immediately sold twenty. Later, schools also bought them to use in language development.

After a visit to the United States in 1952, Ibuka made plans to take out a licence on a new device called a transistor, which would replace bulky hot vacuum tubes, and enable them to make a radio small enough to go into a shirt pocket. The first successfully commercialized transistorized radio was produced in 1955 and the pocket-sized one in 1957. Later, their inventions included the development of transistorized televisions, the world's first video cassette recorder for home use and 8-mm video, CD players and now MiniDisc.

The company's name was Tokyo Tsushin Kogyo Kabushiki Kaisha – a new short name was needed, with only four or five characters, one which would not only be recognized but could be pronounced anywhere in the world. Eventually they came across 'sonus', a Latin word meaning sound; another alternative was 'sonny' or 'sonny boy' – they were bright optimistic sounds but, unfortunately, 'sonny' in Japanese would be pronounced 'shn-nee', which means to lose money – not a good idea to launch a product! They pondered on the question and there it was – 'SONY'. The name is the logo.

Over the years, Sony has progressed in many ways, but has perhaps become most famous for the 'Walkman'. Ibuka liked listening to music, but did not want to disturb other people. Akio arranged for the removal of the recording circuit and speaker from a small cassette recorder and replaced them with a stereo amplifier and lightweight headphones. Nobody liked the name 'Walkman', but Akio was determined and eventually he called up Sony America and Sony UK and said, 'This is an order; the name is "Walkman"!' – and the world has shared his enthusiasm.

ABOVE LEFT: *Sony Walkman, 1979*

FACING PAGE, LEFT: *1954 advertisement*
FACING PAGE, TOP RIGHT: *A light-hearted advertisement*
FACING PAGE, BELOW RIGHT: *Jacob Spear*

SPEAR'S GAMES ®

DONT HAVE WORDS—

HAVE **SCRABBLE**

The LAST WORD in GAMES

When Jacob Spear made his first inlaid chess board, little did he know that later he would be founding a company which was to become one of the world's best-known game manufacturing firms. It was in 1878 that Jacob started his import and wholesale business, in Eldon Street, London. The following year, he decided to move to Nurnberg in Germany, which at that time was regarded as the toy capital of Europe. There he set up a manufacturing unit, but he still retained a sales office in England. As early as 1895, Spear was exporting games to Japan.

Jacob Spear had a large family, and four of his sons became his partners at some time. However, it was Carl who took over after his father's death in 1893, and built up the business into one of the foremost games manufacturers in Germany.

In 1932, the Nurnberg factory found it was not in a position to compete in the United Kingdom market and it was decided to send Richard Spear, son of Carl, and now a partner in the firm, back to England to establish a manufacturing unit. Richard chose a site in Enfield, in suburban London, and, with a staff of twenty, opened the factory. Gradually, the enterprise grew until the Second World War disrupted production and overseas markets closed. After the war growth resumed, a neighbouring site was acquired, and a new factory built.

During the Depression in America, Alfred Butts, a temporarily unemployed New York architect, had an idea for a game, which he enjoyed playing with his wife and friends, and he developed it between 1933 and 1948. It was a word-based game which had several names during its early years, ranging from 'Alph' and 'It' to 'Lexiko'. In the earliest version of Lexiko there were no racks and no playing board. Although the

game was enjoyed by Butts's friends, when it was sent to games manufacturers no one was interested in producing it. Later he devised a board and had the idea that it be played like a crossword – and still no manufacturer was interested.

In 1939, Alfred Butts met James Brunot, a government social worker, and showed him his game, which he then called Criss-Crosswords. After the war, Brunot and a partner contacted Butts to discuss the possible marketing and production of this game. Brunot approached a trademark agent and, from a list of names which the agent suggested, he chose 'Scrabble'. Scrabble was introduced in 1948.

In the first year, 2,250 sets were sold, but the company still made a loss, and it was 1952 before they started to make a profit. During the summer of that year the game took off, and by 1954 over four million sets had been sold. Jack Strauss, the chairman of Macy's department store in New York, had played Scrabble on holiday with friends and, on returning to work, was amazed to find that Macy's did not stock the game. He immediately placed a large order with Brunot and promoted the game in the store.

In 1953, Scrabble started selling in Australia and from there it gradually spread worldwide.

J W Spear & Sons Ltd introduced Scrabble to Great Britain in 1954, and in 1969 they acquired the worldwide rights for the game, outside the United States, Canada and Australia. Today, the game is played in many languages throughout the world, and for blind people there is a Braille version.

In the 1970s, J W Spear increased its range of products when it acquired the firm of G J Hayter & Co Ltd, makers of the famous Victory wooden jigsaw puzzles. Spear's are still on the lookout for new ideas and each year introduce games suitable for different ages and interests.

ABOVE LEFT AND RIGHT: *Early Spears toys*

FACING PAGE, TOP: *Advertisement from the turn of the century*
FACING PAGE, BELOW: *Showcard from the 1920s*

The 'jolly miller', once a familiar figure in towns and villages, was generally big in brawn and bone for he had to hump sacks of flour, weighing 280lbs, around the mill.

Joel Spiller was born in Bridgwater, Somerset, in 1804, the son of an ironmonger with Flemish origins. Bridgwater was a busy trading centre, and ships from many countries unloaded at its quayside. Transport was by horse and cart, the post coach, the canal barge or the coastal vessel. Most food was home-grown and there were import taxes on grain. The milling process was a tradition handed down from father to son, but the passing of a law in 1815, allowing corn to be imported, brought changes.

In 1829, Joel Spiller started business as a 'Corn Factor and Dealer' in St Mary Street, Bridgwater; later that year he married Sarah Taylor Durston at nearby St Mary's Church. As imports increased, and harvests at home were good, business prospered. In 1840, Spiller went into partnership with Samuel Woolcott Browne, son of Captain Charles Browne RN, who had sailed with Nelson, and was now one of Bridgwater's bankers. They built a four-storey warehouse on the West Quay and had an office in fashionable Castle Street. Joel Spiller, by now a man of influence in this fast-growing town, had a house in Northgate, near to the office, quay and new dock. Spiller and Browne built their first steam-powered mill in Chilton Street, about a mile out of town but only about a hundred yards from the river.

The Corn Laws were repealed in 1846 and immediately the partners sought to expand. They rented three watermills in Somerset, but also looked across the Bristol Channel to Cardiff. Some local people sailed for Canada, settling in the wheatlands of the mid-West and sent back grain on the returning empty emigrant ships. As the coalfields opened up in the Welsh valleys, Spiller supplied flour to the miners and their families.

In 1852, Spiller leased a site from the Marquess of Bute, on the West Dock at Cardiff, to build a mill larger than anything he could have visualized at Bridgwater. On

one of his frequent visits to the mill during its construction, in June 1853, he grazed his shin. Although the injury seemed slight, the wound turned septic and he died shortly after, leaving a wife and three children; he was only forty-nine. His commercial judgement had been acute and imaginative, and was therefore the architect of his own success; he was also remembered as a fine family man and friend.

After Joel Spiller's death, Samuel Woolcott Browne brought his brother-in-law Charles Thompson, and Joel Spiller's brother-in-law William Allen, into the business. Browne negotiated a contract to supply flour to British troops fighting in the Crimea, but, after the war ended, the partners took an old Cardiff bakery and supplied ships with kiln-dried flour and ship's biscuits. In 1855, they also started to make dog biscuits. Then, in 1860, Spillers headquarters moved to Cardiff's Bute Street. At that time, wheat was imported from Russia, Germany and France, although most was grown in Britain.

In the 1870s, the company's younger management team moved it forward into a new technological age, and by 1877 it was producing 4,000 sacks of flour each week, much of it processed through the new steel roller mills; by 1879 this had risen to 10,000 sacks. That year was disastrous for the English wheat harvest but, as a result, Spillers started a new trade in grain. Over the next few years it expanded into the Midlands and down to Devon and Cornwall. By 1885, the Cardiff mills were turning out 25,000 sacks of corn produce a week. In 1887, the business went public when Spiller & Company (Cardiff) Ltd was launched with paid-up capital of £440,000. The founding directors were all members of the Allen and Thompson families. After the firm's incorporation, employees were allowed to buy shares 'to participate directly in its prosperity'. Two years later they were offered a profit-sharing scheme, but turned it down.

William Edgar Nicholls, who negotiated the company's amalgamation with its rivals, William Baker & Sons of Bristol, in 1891, eventually became managing director, and later chairman. In 1920, he was knighted.

By the turn of the century, the growing company had agencies in Paris, New York, Cape Town, Switzerland and Argentina, and 1903 saw the launching of a brown flour which made 'the perfect loaf of best brown bread, moist but not stodgy, light in crumb but not crumbly'. At first it was named 'Twrog', after a Welsh hero, but was later anglicized to 'Turog'. Following a large advertising campaign, Turog became such big business that a subsidiary company, Turog Brown Flour Company, was formed.

The company expanded into agricultural and domestic animal foods such as Saval puppy food, Spillers Shapes and Winalot dog food; diversification was now real and in 1916 the head offices were moved to London.

Following a visit to Canada in 1923, Sir William Nicholls said, 'I look on Canada as the granary of the Empire', and, in 1924, the company acquired the Vancouver Terminal Grain Company Ltd.

Then came 1926, a bleak year for the company, which made a serious loss. Nicholls

Keep fit on
TUROG
BREAD

BELOW RIGHT: *Early advertisement*

resigned after being managing director for thirty-five years and chairman for twenty. Every subsidiary company was liquidated and assets were concentrated in the parent company which became Spillers Limited.

Following the bleak years of the 1920s, the 1930s was a time for consolidation and expansion; old mills were replaced by new ones at deep-water ports and rival firms were taken over. Over the years the quality of the flour improved as technology allowed the floury parts inside the wheat to be extracted from the husk, giving a pure white flour. Bulk handling of flour in large road tankers, and the grading of flour by sieving were yet to come.

United Bakeries, a subsidiary company, was set up in 1955 and gradually new bakeries were added, producing 'Wonder' bread and cakes.

In 1960, Spillers bought Spratts Patent Limited, well-known makers of pet foods, and the acquisition, in 1964, of Scottish Animal Products Ltd gave them the Kattomeat and Kennomeat brands. Arthur, the loving white cat, also appeared, and later gave his name to his own brand, 'Arthur's'.

A new mill was opened at Gainsborough, Lincolnshire, in 1962, and shortly afterwards Spillers launched 'Homepride' flour; this had actually been introduced in 1924 by Paul Brothers, a company Spillers took over in 1945, but now, marketed intensively, it became a brand leader. Television commercials were launched in 1965, after two

advertising executives visited the Avonmouth Mill. They watched the grains being graded and the slogan 'Graded grains make finer flour' resulted, along with Fred the little bowler-hatted cartoon flour grader, who soon became a family favourite.

After further diversification, the acquisition of 'Tyne Brand', in 1967, took Spillers into food canning. New brands of pet foods, Top Cat, Top Dog and Choosy appeared in 1969, and the company opened its own Nutritional Centre at Kennett, near Newmarket. Three years later it acquired the pet food business of Rank Hovis McDougall. In 1970, Sainsbury-Spillers Ltd was formed to run chicken processing plants and egg packing stations, based on Spillers' feeds.

After amalgamations and mergers in 1972, Spillers owned twenty-eight per cent of the milling industry and twenty per cent of the baking industry in Britain. Homepride Bakeries was created to give regional pride in the products of individual bakeries, and Spillers Farm Feeds, Spillers Horse Feeds and Spillers Foods for pets also became brand leaders.

Today, Spillers is an international company, at the forefront of food production and of specialist animal feeds for both the farmer and the pet owner. In 1979, the company became part of Dalgety.

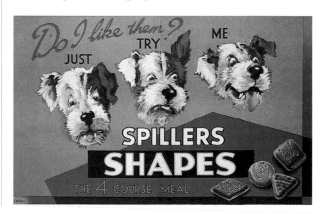

James Spratt was born in Devon about 1809, possibly in the Exeter area. He always claimed to be the son of a James Spratt, naval officer, although there is some doubt about this. His first wife, Elizabeth, came from Clerkenwell, London, but, by 1840, he and Elizabeth were living in Whitewater, Ohio, in the United States, together with a little boy.

While in America, James invented the Mason Fruit Jar and also tips for lightning-conductors. He became friendly with a family named Walton, and during the terrible cholera epidemic of 1849 both the Walton

parents died, leaving seven children who were all quarantined from May to December of that year. During that time, James Spratt looked after the children, later adopting the two-year-old daughter, Alice. What happened to the boy – and who he actually was – remains a mystery. James's official occupation was then 'Lightning-Rod Maker'.

In the late 1850s, James Spratt left the United States, anticipating the American Civil War. A Mr Elphy kept a noted ham and beef shop at Middle Row, Holborn, London, and when he died the premises were let to James who tried to sell his lightning-conductors, with little success.

In 1859, a James Tayler was born to a single girl, Ellen Tayler. He was in fact the illegitimate son of James Spratt. After his wife's death in 1872, from 'softening of the brain', Spratt married Ellen, who was about thirty years his junior, and the daughter of Admiral James Needham Tayler, RN. James Tayler became James Spratt jnr.

Following the abolition of bull and bear baiting, dog breeding and showing became a popular hobby, but many dogs in London

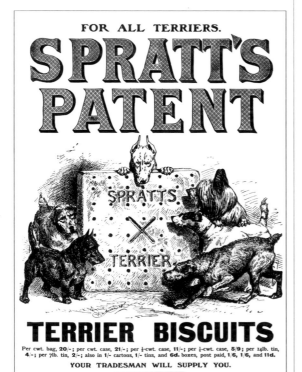

FOR ALL TERRIERS.

SPRATT'S PATENT

SPRATTS X TERRIER

TERRIER BISCUITS

Per cwt. bag, 20/-; per cwt. case, 21/-; per ½-cwt. case, 11/-; per ¼-cwt. case, 5/9; per 14lb. tin, 4/-; per 7lb. tin, 2/-; also in 1/- cartons, 1/- tins, and 6d. boxes, post paid, 1/6, 1/6, and 11d.

YOUR TRADESMAN WILL SUPPLY YOU.

SEND POSTCARD FOR PAMPHLET ON KENNEL MANAGEMENT, POST FREE OF

SPRATT'S PATENT, Ltd.,
24 and 25, Fenchurch Street, LONDON, E.C.

LEFT: *Advertisement from 1907*
ABOVE: *Advertisement in* Picture Post, *1955*
FACING PAGE, LEFT: Tailwagger *magazine, 1945*
FACING PAGE, RIGHT: *1952 advertisement*

were fed on weevily biscuits, discarded by returning ships.

A letter from one of Alice Walton Spratt's brothers describes how, in 1862, James Spratt, in the company of the Waltons' grandfather, visited Sir Richard Herring's farm where he saw foxhounds and met their keeper. James asked what the dogs' food consisted of. Shortly after this, he started manufacturing dog biscuits and took out a provisional patent for them in November 1861. He called his large square dog biscuits 'Spratts Meat Fibrine Dog Cake'. They remained in production for nearly a hundred years.

James obtained some dried buffalo meat and also bought a quantity of old ships' biscuits and dried beef, the latter looking more like mahogany, it having been left over after some clippers and Australian ships had returned. James is said to have ground the biscuits in a mill, similar to a coffee grinder, and the meat was soaked and lightly boiled in the copper in the basement of the shop, which had previously been used for boiling the 'noted ham and beef'.

In his provisional specification, titled 'Preparation of Food for Hogs &c.' he describes the process thus: 'First, I crush, pound, grind, or pulverize the articles known as greaves, dregs, scraps, the same being the residue left after the boiling down of animals, or portions thereof, or of rough fat from tallow chandlers, fat melters, or butcher's trimmings, and other such like matters.' To this he then added various flour, meal and other farinaceous materials, before baking it into biscuits or bread. In some recipes, he also added charcoal to correct acidity or other 'morbid conditions of the stomach', whereas for poultry he would add bone and lime, or preferably oyster shell, this being pounded with a suitable portion of sulphur, capsicum, pepper or spice.

Spratt quickly made his fortune and, in 1866, he engaged a bright fourteen-year-old boy, Charles Cruft, who became his chief sales representative. It is said that Charles's basic method of book-keeping led to the adoption of the St Andrew's Cross as a trademark – he used an X in the ledger to distinguish the trade buyers from the private buyers. Today we remember Cruft because of the dog show which he organized and managed. In 1868, Spratt also obtained an exclusive licence for a food for horses. By 1870, Spratt had been bought out by Edward and Charles Wylam, and Edward's brother-in-law George Beetham Batchelor.

They formed Spratts Patent Ltd, and built a factory near London Bridge.

James Spratt lived at Horsted Keynes in Sussex, at a farm he referred to as 'Sprattville'. In 1879, he went to Nice 'for his health' and died there in January 1880. There is no indication that James Spratt jnr played any part in the business.

To cope with worldwide demand for its products a huge factory, the largest of its kind in the world, was opened in Poplar in 1904. In 1907, it introduced 'Mixed Ovals'. Other factory premises were also opened in New York and at Newark, New Jersey. During the First World War, Spratts baked over 1.2 billion biscuits for the forces.

Spratts later diversified into producing laboratory equipment, bird cages, boarding kennels, advisory leaflets, stationery for pet shows, and also established a livestock shipping department which arranged the transportation of both domestic and exotic species, from cats to giant tortoises, around the world. It was said that to travel via Spratts was 'to the dumb creation, what travelling via Pullman is to human beings'.

Spratts also supplied such famous expeditions as Captain Scott's and Sir Ernest Shackleton's with food for their sledge huskies.

In 1928, Captain Horatio Hobbs, Spratts Advertising Manager, became involved with National Dog Week and, later that year, formed the Tailwaggers Club. By the mid-1930s, the club had half a million members.

Competition with Spillers intensified over the years; Spillers introduced 'Shapes' and 'Winalot', but, in 1932, Spratts retaliated with 'Bonio', the 'bone-shaped biscuit for the dog-shaped dog'. In 1934, it absorbed Caperns, a competitor in the bird food market.

Spratts first tinned product, Spratts Meat for Dogs, was introduced in 1950, using whale meat from carcasses which had been discarded once the blubber had been removed. Other products included Spratts Fish and Top Cat.

In 1960, Spillers bought the whole of Spratts enterprises for £4 million. The Tailwaggers Club continued to receive substantial legacies and Spillers established the Tailwaggers Club Trust until the Club itself closed in 1975. The name of Spratts lives on in some of Spillers product range. Spillers became part of Dalgety in 1979.

ABOVE LEFT: *Pet shop in Sheffield, 1956*

FACING PAGE, RIGHT: *Advertisement from 1954*

The Van den Bergh family takes its name from 's Heerenberg, a Dutch village known in common parlance as Den Bergh. In the eighteenth century, the family set up home in Geffen, in the Brabant region of Holland, near to Oss where there was a thriving butter market.

Simon Van den Bergh was born in Geffen in 1819. He became a small, delicate, good-looking lad, with black curly hair, but he had a pronounced limp. He was not a particularly dynamic man, but kindly and simple in his tastes. In 1844, he married his cousin, Elizabeth Van der Wielen, and it is probable that their children got their energy and motivation from their mother, for Elizabeth was a spirited woman.

The Van den Bergh enterprise started in bartering groceries and dry goods for local butter, which was then resold in Amsterdam and Rotterdam. In order to be better placed to carry out their butter trading, Simon moved with his wife and five sons to live in Oss in 1858. The Van den Berghs were a hard-working and clean-living family, but Oss was a lawless town where their trade rivals, the Jurgens family, lived.

Simon intended to start exporting butter to London, but knew nothing of England or its markets, and soon he was in deep trouble as those in Amsterdam and Rotterdam also suffered from severe price fluctuations. In 1868, the family had to suspend payments to their creditors – not a good start.

However, Elizabeth persuaded their creditors to accept a ten per cent composition until things improved and she then set about reorganizing the business. One of her first decisions was to send their two older sons, Jacob and Henry, to England to investigate the butter market. Although they were only twenty and seventeen years old respectively, they took the place of the agents and looked after the family interests in London. Now that the family knew the retail price of butter, they could decide an appropriate wholesale price to charge.

In 1870, Henry and his father started buying butter from Germany, Switzerland and Italy, and mixed it with Dutch butter before selling it on the London market. Soon the brothers were also supplying the provinces.

During that period, the English standard of living was low: many people could not

YOU'VE BEEN PATIENT – YOU'VE 'MADE DO' LONG ENOUGH!

Soon you'll have Stork!

you're going to love its creamy taste!

Only a little longer to wait! Then it's good-bye to those dreary years of making do—and all set for your first exciting taste of fresh creamy Stork! Yes, your *first* taste! Because even if you knew Stork Margarine back in the old days, you'll find Stork now *unbelievably* creamy—*with all the flavour of fresh country produce*. It's the cream of natural fats . . . sunshine in vitamin form . . . and milk — churned into a smooth, delicious blend of golden goodness.

SOON YOU'LL BE SAYING:

"FANCY CALLING STORK MARGARINE!"

VAN DEN BERGHS & JURGENS LIMITED, LONDON, E.C.1

afford butter and their diet lacked adequate levels of fat. A cheap butter substitute was needed. In France, in 1869, Napoleon III stimulated the search for such a product by promoting a competition among chemists, and Mège Mouriés produced the best formula. It was a combination of oil of kidney fat churned with milk and sliced udders!

The 'Margarine', or 'Butterine', industry was first developed in Holland, in the 1870s and 1880s, as they had plentiful supplies of the raw materials, and also saw the potential of the product. Aware that their rivals, the Jurgens, were successfully producing margarine, the Van den Berghs set up a factory in Oss which was operating before the end of 1872. Initially, the Jurgens had taken control of most of the raw materials and this impeded the progress of the Van den Berghs, but, when supplies started coming from North America towards the end of the decade, the family firm was again ready for expansion. However, it still lacked capital.

By 1885, Simon had retired and the sons ran the business. Jacob was the financial genius and he did not retire until he was eighty; Henry was an ambitious and keen salesman, and these two took the lead, but were later joined by brothers Isaac, Arnold and Sam. In 1895, the company went public in London, as it was easier to raise capital from there.

Gradually, the brothers built strong relationships with the new multiple retail grocery stores which were developing throughout Britain, acquiring financial interests in several of them. In 1905 and 1906, they took shares in some of these companies on the understanding that they sold only Van den Bergh margarine and no other. These links enabled them to promote a specific branded, packed, fixed-price margarine direct to shops.

Production of margarine still remained in Holland, although the base was moved nearer to England, to Rotterdam. They had trained research chemists and, by 1906, were selling twice as much margarine in Britain as Jurgens, their nearest rival.

Aware of the problems that might be caused by the importing of colonial butter, the Van den Berghs diversified by using the by-products from the manufacturing process. Skimmed milk was used for condensed milk, but a by-product from this was cream, which was used to make butter. Other ventures included the supply of Danish bacon, and also the making of soap, which used up waste fats from the margarine process.

FACING PAGE, TOP: *An advertisement featuring the stork* FACING PAGE, BELOW, AND THIS PAGE, RIGHT: *Pre-war advertising signs* BELOW RIGHT: *Cut-out poster*

As butter supplies grew, margarine values dropped and, in 1908, the Van den Berghs and Jurgens made a pooling agreement whereby profits of the two companies were shared, sixty per cent to Van den Berghs and forty per cent to Jurgens – it was the first international cartel in the margarine industry. Unfortunately, the agreement was not satisfactory and in 1914 it was suspended. During the war, Van den Bergh introduced its Blue Band brand which became very popular. In 1918, when the Dutch government banned exports, production for the British market had to be moved to a factory in Fulham. In 1920, Jurgens introduced Stork margarine into Britain; they had registered the trademark in London in 1900.

In 1927, a merger took place between Van den Bergh and Jurgens. Two holding companies were formed: a Dutch company, the Margarine Unie NV; and the British, Margarine Union Ltd, both with identical boards. These new companies, with Lever Brothers, were the greatest powers in the European oils and fats industry. Only two years later, they came together to form Unilever.

In 1934, a bronze tablet was unveiled at the Stork margarine works at Purfleet in Essex by Frans Jurgens and J P Van den Bergh, two of the great-grandsons of the first manufacturers of the industry; it celebrated Mège Mouriés, the inventor of margarine.

By 1937, Unilever was producing nearly 40,000 tons of Stork margarine and it was advertised on Radio Luxembourg's 'Stork Radio Parade'. During the Second World War, to keep the brand name alive during a period when brands were suspended, Unilever introduced 'The Stork Cookery Service'. Even in 1946 they had to use the slogan, 'Stork will be back one day', for food rationing had still not ended. In 1957, the 'Can You Tell the Difference?' campaign was launched and, by 1960, Stork had a forty-three per cent share of the margarine market. Stork Soft tub margarine was introduced in 1970.

In 1995, Stork celebrated its seventy-fifth year and Stork Rich Blend was introduced. Today, Van den Bergh Foods, now incorporating Brooke Bond Foods, both subsidiaries of Unilever, employs over 3,000 people and has an annual turnover of £800 million. It brings together such well-known names as Colman's, Oxo, Batchelors, Flora, PG Tips, Jiff Lemon, Krona, I Can't Believe It's Not Butter . . . and, of course, Stork!

FREE GIFTS FROM STORK MARGARINE

Arthur Charles Wilkin was born in 1835 at Trewlands in the village of Tiptree, near Colchester in Essex. As a lad of fifteen, he went to work in London as an office boy, but desperately missed the green fields, fresh air and freedom of home. He worked in the hosiery trade and became a strong Non-Conformist, a radical Liberal, a Temperance advocate, and a firm exponent of scrupulously honest principles. At the age of twenty-four, after working on several farms, he returned home to work with his father and eventually rented ten acres from him to grow mangold seed.

Arthur Wilkin's parents encouraged him to take over the farm and he started to specialize in fruit production. During a local evangelistic revival, he, along with the local pastor, visited a farmer in nearby Coggeshall to collect money towards the building of a Congregational Church; he also met the farmer's daughter whom he later married.

In the mid-1860s, Arthur started growing strawberries, raspberries and blackcurrants. Having difficulty in obtaining plants, he discussed the matter with Mr Blackwell, then senior partner in Crosse and Blackwell, who drew him into a group of growers with whom he did business.

He started supplying strawberries to London jam makers, but with little help from the railway staff, who insisted on transporting the fruit in coal trucks covered with black tarpaulins which spoilt the fruit. So bad were the problems, he nearly gave up the fruit business.

At the age of forty-eight, with a wife, three sons and two daughters, he felt 'it was

LEFT: *Boiling Room, c. 1920*
ABOVE: *Arthur Wilkin*
FACING PAGE, TOP: *Mrs A C Wilkin (aged ninety) in 1926*
FACING PAGE, BELOW: *Advertisement from the turn of the century*

about time to pull himself together and consider that if he was ever going to do anything in life there was no time to lose'. About this time, Mr Gladstone, the Prime Minister, made a speech encouraging his tenants to grow fruit and make jam. The comments were said to have caused some ridicule in agricultural circles, but Arthur, along with friends Edward Basden and B A Smith, formed a small private company. Mr Smith sent a first-rate jam maker down from London, and also introduced an Australian merchant who agreed to take all the whole-fruit strawberry jam that the company could make. He insisted that the jam should be free from glucose, colouring matter and preservatives and be called 'Conserve', to distinguish it from poorer products. Also, it should bear the name 'Britannia Preserving Company', Britannia being a good trading name for Australia.

The first jam was made in Mrs Wilkin's kitchen, using her recipes. Arthur acquired three boiling pans but, as he could not afford a boiler, he hired two traction engines which normally worked a threshing machine, stood them outside the barn and linked the power to the pans inside. He sent Mr Gladstone a box of strawberry jam and in return received an encouraging letter. On 1 April 1888, Arthur Wilkin became Managing Director of the Britannia Fruit Preserving Co Ltd.

The company had 238 acres of land, including 100 acres of strawberries, raspberries and other fruits. During that first summer, it made fewer than fifty tons of conserves, jams, jellies and bottled fruits. The partners did not approve of retail trade and appointed travellers to sell their goods, but, due to heavy expenses and bad debts, there was a deficit of £1,800 at the end of 1888. Arthur wrote: 'It needed a lion's heart to go on.'

Nevertheless, he did go on and, subsidized by the fruit farm, the jam-making continued.

In 1892, he invited sixty-two Salvationists to come from the Leigh Farm Colony and pick strawberries. So impressed was he by their behaviour and religious meetings, he persuaded the Congregational Church to invite the Salvation Army to establish a Corps in Tiptree which opened in 1906, strongly supported by Arthur.

Mechanization was introduced to carry out orange-slicing, gooseberry-topping, currant-stalking and bottle-corking. During a particularly busy period in 1896, the pans boiled strawberry jam night and day for a week without a stop! By the start of the new century, the company had over 8,000 customers, including the royal household at Windsor Castle and Osborne House, and special packagings of conserves were being sent to the tropics.

Picking of strawberries commenced at 4am, the first lot being made into jam by 6.15am. By now, the range of fruit had been

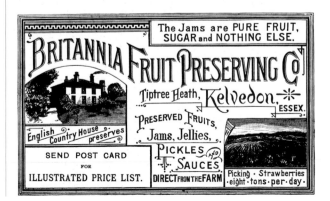

LEFT: *Early Britannia label*
BELOW: *Advertisement from* Woman's Journal, *1984*

FACING PAGE, TOP RIGHT: *1950s' advertisement*
FACING PAGE, LEFT: *A very early advertisement*
FACING PAGE, BELOW RIGHT: *From the 'Out of School' series*

extended to include greengage, black-currant, damson and gooseberry; five different types of marmalade were also produced, plus a range of pickles, fruit in syrups and jelly, and varied sauces and vinegars.

Before the introduction of the State pension in 1911, Arthur and some friends were so concerned at the low level of Poor Relief that they developed a scheme to help the poor of the Maldon district of Essex. Over a twelve-year period, £4,651 5s 6d was distributed, and altogether the company built 100 houses for its employees.

With twenty companies trading under the Britannia name in 1905, it was decided to have a trademark, 'Tiptree', and name the company 'Wilkin & Sons Ltd'. At this

time, it was not unusual for a thousand men, women and children to be involved in picking the fruit at any one time.

The company received its first Royal Warrant in 1911 from George V, and today still holds a Royal Warrant for jam and marmalade. In that year, it also supplied the royal families of Russia, Spain, Sweden and Greece. Arthur Wilkin died in 1913; his widow lived on until 1933.

During the Second World War, the government insisted that the bitter orange content of Wilkin's marmalade be restricted to twelve per cent and so the company named it Unitree, to avoid devaluing the Tiptree reputation. In 1964 came the introduction of ¾lb jars with twist-off caps to replace the 1lb ones with push-off lids. This decade also saw big increases in export sales, particularly to America and West Germany.

The company has kept abreast of modern technology and ensured its position as a manufacturer and supplier of quality conserves to the world. Trewlands, Arthur Wilkin's birthplace, is now part of the works complex, and still of importance is Arthur Wilkin's 'Little Scarlet Strawberry', a wild strawberry from which the conserve of the same name is made. Today, Tiptree remains a family business and is proud of the eighty-seven conserves, marmalades, honeys, chutneys and other preserves it manufactures. Each day, a 'Tasting Time' takes place to ensure the previous day's work has met the required high standard.

TY·PHOO

In 1820, twenty-four-year-old William Sumner took over an old family grocery and druggist's shop at the top of the Bull Ring in Birmingham. Ten years later, William also had a shop in nearby Coleshill and, in 1835, he is listed as a Grocer & Tea Dealer in the *National Commercial Directory*. All the tea sold at that time came from China.

William brought his elder son, John, into the business in 1845, but he had probably already worked in the shop for several years. By 1852, William Sumner & Son were listed as tea and coffee dealers, but it would be many years before they could concentrate solely on tea.

William later gave the business to his two sons, but, in 1863, they decided to go their separate ways and John took premises at 98 High Street, Birmingham.

In Ceylon, now Sri Lanka, a serious disease affected the coffee industry and tea became a prime crop. By 1875, tea was being exported to Britain and this was to be important to the Sumners. John Sumner's son, also John, joined the business but, due to the construction of a railway tunnel, they had to move to 25 and 26 High Street, Birmingham.

At the turn of the century, father and son had a flourishing business which now included wines and spirits, stout and cider, as well as groceries. They had six travellers and twenty horses and a range of vans – life was good.

For a long time Mary, young John's sister, had suffered from indigestion. One day someone sent her a packet of tea which was different from that sold in the family business. Its particles were very small and, whereas large-leaf teas tended to aggravate her problem, this one promised a cure. She decided to try it and to her delight found that it gave her great relief; she then offered the 'remedy' to other people who suffered from indigestion and they too benefited.

Mary told her brother enthusiastically about the tea and asked why Sumner did not sell it. This was the starting point of a great adventure, although when John told a friend, a wholesale tea merchant, of his intention to buy thirty chests of the tea, he said that the public would not buy tea which looked little better than dust. Nevertheless John went ahead with his purchase, but, instead of selling it loose over the counter, he decided to put it in packets and sell it under a brand name.

John set himself three criteria in choosing

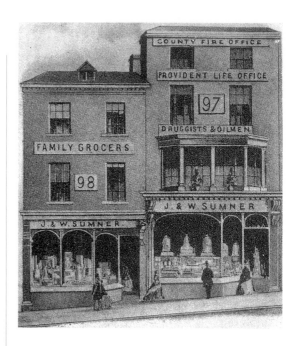

the name: it must be distinctive and unlike others; it must be one which tripped off the tongue; and it must be one which could be protected by registration. Finally, he came up with the name 'Ty-Phoo' Tipps – it had an oriental sound, was alliterative with tea, and whilst the name Tipps could not be registered Ty-Phoo could and was. The 'pp' in Tipps first occurred as a printer's error.

The first cardboard packets were filled by girls using scoops, who then weighed them, before glueing and sealing them. In the first week of production in 1903, they packed 577lbs of Ty-Phoo Tipps. To encourage customers to buy his new brand, John offered each purchaser of 1lb of Ty-Phoo Tipps a generous jar of cream. Soon many customers were drinking the new tea. They discovered that, although it was slightly

more expensive, it was more economical and its beneficial digestive qualities gave it great appeal. Other traders also wanted the new brand and John founded a wholesale agency.

He took a shop in Corporation Street, Birmingham's most important shopping street, and had a row of girls standing inside the window, packing tea for passers-by to see, whilst inside the shop tea was served with cream and biscuits.

For over thirty years, the Sumners had enjoyed the confidence of the bank manager, even though they had a large overdraft, but now they needed new capital. A new manager had come to the bank and, instead of approving another loan, as John had expected, he called in the overdraft monies and offered no help. It was a time of crisis.

A quick decision was needed – John felt the new tea business was on the brink of success, so he backed his intuition, sold the grocery business carefully built up by his father and grandfather and put his faith in Ty-Phoo. On selling the grocery business he repaid the bank and immediately closed his account with them. The bank had lost a major customer.

In July 1905, Sumner's Ty-Phoo Tea Ltd was incorporated and that year John went to Ceylon and brought back 200 chests of tea, mainly the small-leafed variety known as fannings. He drew attention to the fact that his tea came from the edge of the leaf and did not contain the tannin from the

fibrous stalk; he also claimed that the leaf-edge tea could produce eighty more cups per pound of tea than the large-leaf teas. He enlisted the support of doctors to confirm that his tea relieved dyspepsia.

From 1906, John Sumner was having his own special Ty-Phoo patent teapots made for sale, and during that year he introduced picture cards, similar to cigarette cards, and inserted them in the packets of tea.

By 1909, he had repaid all his debts and again owned most of the shares. Now he could make a visit to Ceylon to establish closer relationships with the growers and blenders. He arranged for the tea to be blended in Ceylon and for it to be packed into 70lb chests; the chest size was important because, when the tea had been packeted, they could be reused to hold exactly 50lbs of tea for distribution to wholesalers. When the chests arrived in Birmingham they were carefully opened with claw hammers, and the nails were reused when the packeted tea was dispatched in the same chests, thus saving a few more pence.

By 1919, orders received in the morning were generally dispatched the same day, and by 1927 Ty-Phoo tea was being exported.

FACING PAGE, TOP LEFT: *Sir John Sumner*
FACING PAGE, BELOW LEFT: *A 1917 half-pound pack*
FACING PAGE, TOP RIGHT: *Premises at 98 High Street, Birmingham*
TOP: *Early Ty-Phoo teabags*
RIGHT: *1950s' advertisement*

In 1932, John Sumner received a knighthood in recognition of his philanthropic work. When he died in 1934, each of his 346 employees benefited under his will.

During the Second World War, the works were destroyed by bombs in 1941, but arrangements were made for a special 'Emergency Blend', which was packed by Brooke Bond Ltd and Lyons Ltd, a gesture much appreciated by Ty-Phoo. In December 1941, the company became Ty-Phoo Tea Ltd.

In 1968, Ty-Phoo Schweppes was formed. This was enlarged in 1969, when Kenco Coffee became part of Schweppes, and when Schweppes and Cadbury came together. In 1986, following a management buyout, Premier Brands Ltd was launched which later acquired Ridgways, a long-established tea company, and also the London Herb & Spice Co, the leading name in herbal teas.

UHU®

Ludwig Hoerth owned a dyeing and cotton printing factory in the small town of Buhl, in the Baden region of Germany. In 1884, he started producing a range of items for use in offices, including inks, water colours, ink pads and their refills, typewriter ribbons, varnishes and glues – he used the brand name 'Ambra'.

August Fischer moved from his native Wurttemberg, with his wife and four children, to live in Buhl in 1905. He bought the Ludwig Hoerth Chemical Factory and soon showed his skills as an entrepreneurial chemist, quickly becoming well known far beyond Germany. The cutting off of Alsace Lorraine and the Saarland from Germany during the First World War and the post-war high inflation and worldwide depression caused them many problems.

Hugo Fischer, August's eldest son, served his apprenticeship in the factory and, in 1924, when he was twenty-four, he took over the commercial management of the firm. This gave August, who was primarily a scientist, more time to concentrate on his experiments in the laboratory. His work centred round the development of a glue which he knew would be superior to any product on the market; he knew how poor some glues were. For almost a decade, Hugo and his devoted workers kept the business together whilst August pursued his research.

In 1932, he formulated a synthetic resin-based, highly transparent adhesive capable of glueing practically anything – it was ideal for use in the home and office as it would stick paper and card, china and ceramics, leather, fabrics and even wood. It was also waterproof, remained elastic and was resistant to the effects of other materials such as acids and petroleum products. Both August and Hugo realized they had a winner – now

LEFT: *UHU factory complex*
FACING PAGE, TOP: *The Eagle Owl or Uhu after which the brand is named*
FACING PAGE, BELOW: *A painting showing early packaging*

they needed a name that was memorable and distinctive.

Following a custom in their industry, which already included such brand names as Pelikan and Schwan, Hugo chose as their heraldic animal a bird of prey, the eagle-owl or uhu, and within a few years UHU had become a generic name for household adhesives. Hugo Fischer started to publicize the new UHU all-purpose adhesive and for five years 36,000 schools all over Germany were provided with samples, as well as many stationers and chemist shops. Gradually, modest advertisements were placed in youth magazines.

Manfred Fischer, August's second son, joined the company in 1936, having studied science and economics. He had also worked in chemo-pharmaceutical companies and had qualified as both a pharmacist and chemist. When the company over-reached itself in financial terms, the two brothers dissolved their father's sole proprietor company, assumed its debts, and went into general partnership as Ludwig Hoerth OHG; August had put his life's work entirely into his sons' hands.

Hugo and Manfred reduced the range of office equipment they sold and concentrated on UHU and related products. In 1938, the company became UHU-Werk Hum Fischer OHG.

A welcome publicity boost came when Count Zeppelin announced that he had used UHU to glue his great airship, the *Hindenburg*. In 1940, August Fischer died; he had been a modest man, a kind and patient listener, and a Buhl district councillor for many years, until the Nazis came to power. Throughout his life he had been a committed Christian, dedicated to his wife and seven children.

In 1949, the foundations were laid for a new factory, and, in 1957, the company

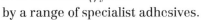

introduced the first proprietary foam bath in the world, Badedas, a vitalizing gel based on horse chestnuts. The next year, they introduced Kontact 2000, their first contact adhesive, which was followed over succeeding years by a range of specialist adhesives.

Hugo Fischer died in 1964, only a few days after he had been made a Freeman of Buhl; he was posthumously awarded the Order of the Federal Republic of Germany. In 1969, UHU introduced the first glue stick.

In 1970, the company became part of SmithKline Beecham, and the phrase 'Don't say Glue, Say UHU!' was introduced in the United Kingdom. Since 1991, UHU has been owned by Bolten International. The original formula All Purpose UHU is brand leader in eighteen countries and sold in 123 countries. UHU now produce 184 different formulae of adhesives, giving sales of over 5 million kilos of glue each year! In 1996, they introduced the first multi-purpose extra-strong glue stick.

VICTORY V
FORGED FOR STRENGTH

Nelson, Lancashire, a typical cotton-mill town, takes its name from a public house called The Nelson Inn, which opened its doors in 1805, and was named as a tribute to Lord Nelson after the Battle of Trafalgar. There two cough remedies were created that became known throughout the world – the Victory V gums and lozenges.

Thomas Fryer learnt about the spice trade (spice being an old name for sweets) whilst working in a spice factory in nearby Barrowford although both his father and grandmother had been confectioners. From there, he took a shop

Worth Holding on to, "Victory!"

next door to the Prince of Wales Inn, in Leeds Road, Nelson in 1864. At that time, the variety of sweets was limited – grocers sold acid drops, sugar sticks, love cheeses, humbugs and sugar candy. Many of these were made by travelling confectioners who paid periodical visits to the shops to sell their wares. Thomas Fryer began making cough lozenges, and then, with the coming of cheaper sugar, he made sweets such as striped cushions, Nelson Balls and Nelson Rock, all at a price customers could afford. His venture was successful and soon he built a factory consisting of two floors and an attic, with rooms about 25-feet square.

Fryer took on a man to act as 'pan man', and he himself set out to learn as much as he could about toffee making, becoming an expert at pan work. He employed Kellett Ashton, who came from Chorley, to sell his products. One day, in about 1884, Ashton told his doctor, Edward Smith, about the toffee venture. The doctor was most interested and sent his brother, William Carruthers Smith, to see Thomas Fryer; the outcome

VICTORY GUMS

VICTORY CHLORODYNE AND GUM FACTORY.

was that William became a partner in the business. In the 1880s, Thomas Fryer & Co moved to new premises in Chapel Street, Nelson, and called it Victory Works, also as a tribute to Lord Nelson.

Pinned on the wall of Thomas Fryer's office was a notice although not of his creation: 'A business is like a wheelbarrow; it must be pushed to make it go.' Smith believed he was the man to do the pushing. First-grade raw material had to be bought in, the sweets had to be made, they had to be packed into tins and boxes, and then the finished products had to be sold. There was much planning to do and advertising to be developed. Bit by bit, the premises were extended and a four-storey building was completed in about 1898; it covered two and a quarter acres.

The recipe for the Victory V gums was given to William by Dr Smith. An article written for the *Nelson Leader* in 1924 describes how the 'sugar is pulverized so fine, and forced through such a close mesh of specially prepared silk, that when it leaves the boxed-in machine it is as dry as tinder, puffy as swansdown and smoother than flour. These three machines turn out 30 tons of pulverized sugar a week.' The top room in the factory was the lozenge room: 'Into a hopper was placed 168lbs. of pulverized sugar, linseed, liquorice, and medicinal chlorodyne. [Pure acacia gum forms the base of all Victory V gums.] A lever was pulled, the mixture began to heave and roll about, the brown syrupy liquorice intermingled with the sugar, and in seven minutes

the whole concoction was correctly mixed without being touched by human hand.' The resultant dough was cut up into lumps and flattened out with rolling pins to an inch thick, before being 'forced through rollers like clothes through a mangle, and carried forward to where it was automatically cut, stamped and dropped into trays to be dried off in a stoving room'. The lozenges were then covered in fine granulated sugar before they were dried off, which might take from four to five days, and then packed.

In the 1920s, the company had representatives in every part of the British Isles; they worked from home, covering their area every six weeks. Fryer's also had agents in Canada, Australia, New Zealand, Norway, Finland, Sweden, in the Near East and Far East, and these agents appointed travellers to sell the products.

In 1992, the business was taken over by Scribbans-Kemp and is now part of Ernest Jackson & Co of Crediton, Devon, where the lozenges are now made. This company is a member of the Trebor Bassett Ltd Group.

FACING PAGE, TOP RIGHT: *1915 advertisement*
FACING PAGE, CENTRE: *Thomas Fryer*
FACING PAGE, BELOW: *Chapel Street factory*
ABOVE LEFT: *William Carruthers Smith*
ABOVE RIGHT: *1899 advertisement*
RIGHT: *Advertisement in* Everybody's, *1956*

WILKINSON SWORD

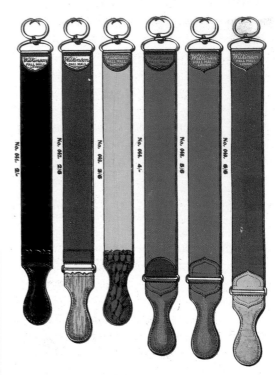

Henry Nock has been described as the greatest gunmaker of his time. He was born in 1741, and started his business in 1772 in Ludgate Street, near St Paul's Cathedral, in London. Over the years he produced top-quality sporting guns, rifles, duelling and target pistols, blunderbusses and other military weapons, including a 7-barrelled volley gun. In 1792, the government gave him a contract, the largest ever placed, for 10,000 flintlock-type muskets and bayonets.

He was an innovative gunmaker and among his inventions was the Nock 'Patent Breech' of 1787, which improved the efficiency of muzzle-loading weapons, the design of sporting guns, and had a major impact on the study of ballistics; from this came the major development of small arms.

Nock became Master of the Worshipful Company of Gunmakers and also received Royal Appointment to George III; since that

time the company has continuously held appointments as gun or sword makers to the British sovereign.

When Nock died in 1804, his partner and son-in-law, James Wilkinson, inherited the business and, when Alexander Forsyth's patent for the percussion system of ignition lapsed in 1820, Wilkinson was one of the first gunmakers to begin using the new system. James Wilkinson's son, Henry, took control of the business in 1825, and it was he who moved the headquarters to 27 Pall Mall, next door to the offices of the Board of Ordnance.

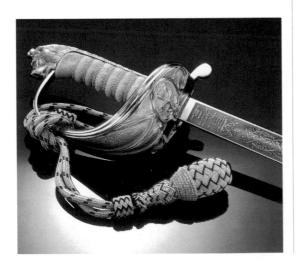

LEFT: *Modern sword handle*
ABOVE: *Razor strops from the turn of the century*
FACING PAGE, TOP RIGHT: *Catalogue entry, c. 1919*
FACING PAGE, BELOW RIGHT: *Presentation swords, c. 1930*

Throughout the nineteenth century, the company made fine guns and swords, having among their customers such famous names as Queen Victoria, the King of Siam, the King of Prussia, Prince N L Bonaparte, and practically every member of the House of Lords. The company continued to be innovative and Henry lectured to the British Institution on the history of weapons of war. He also wrote a book, *Engines of War*, which was published in 1841, and he became a member of the committee of the Great Exhibition of 1851.

Henry was interested in swords and soon became famous for the strength and balance of his military ones. He wrote a book entitled *Observations on Swords*, which ran to twenty-one editions. From 1857, when the government enlarged and modernized its own firearms factory at Enfield Lock, sword making became of greater significance to Wilkinson's. Although Henry was the father of nine children, none succeeded him into the business and, on his death in 1861, he was followed as head of the firm by John Latham who had been with the company since 1845.

In the mid-1880s the 'Great Sword Scandals' hit the headlines. It was suggested that British soldiers in the Sudan were losing their lives due to being armed with inferior swords with blades which bent or snapped whilst in combat. As early as 1844, Wilkinson's had invented a machine for the testing of sword blades and later received an order for the supply of 150,000 sword-bayonets. On the strength of this order, the company built a new factory for the manufacturing of swords and bayonets at Chelsea and, in 1887, it became The Wilkinson Sword Company Ltd. The factory employed about 300 people and turned out 60,000 bayonets and 6,000 swords and lances each year. In 1904,

Wilkinson's produced an experimental sword which, in 1908, became the first purpose-designed trooper sword, but, due to changing military tactics, it became obsolete almost immediately.

When Wilkinson's started to diversify, it was perhaps natural that it should produce the open, or 'cut throat' razor. Then, in about 1898, it produced the 'Pall Mall' safety razor, which was followed by typewriters, bicycles, motorcycles and motor cars, some of which can be seen at the National Motorcycle Museum at Birmingham and at the Wilkinson Sword Centre in London.

During the First World War, the company's factory at Acton produced more than

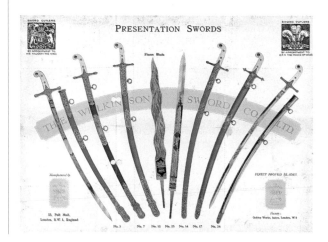

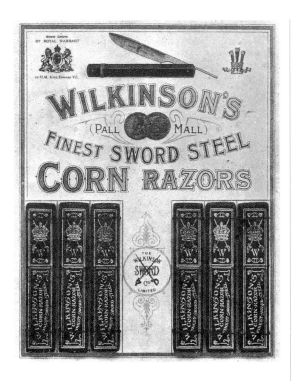

two and a quarter million bayonets as part of the war effort. After the war, Robert Mole of Birmingham, the only other surviving sword makers in England, founded in 1690, became part of Wilkinson's in 1920. That year, Wilkinson's started to manufacture garden tools and has since become well known for these as well as scissors and kitchen knives, which are now produced by Fiskars UK, under licence.

To a large number of men, Wilkinson Sword is still best known for its razors. The Pall Mall had stroppable single-edged blades. Wilkinson's manufactured a special 'stropping machine' into which the blade was

inserted, the leather strop was threaded through the machine and tensioned, and then the machine was pulled back and forth along the strop, which honed the edge at the correct angle. The Empire razor of 1929 had an automatic stropping mechanism, and this continued in production until about 1950. Users were intended to strop the blades regularly, so that they would then last for years. One set, the seven-day set, had blades which were marked for each day of the week. In 1956, Wilkinson Sword entered the double-edge 'wafer' razor-blade market with a stainless steel blade, although they had made 'wafer-blades' before the First World War. This led to the introduction, in 1961, of the PTFE-coated 'Super Sword-Edge' blade and, in 1970, of the Bonded shaving system. Other ranges included the twin-blade units, the swivelling units to follow the contours of the face and, later, the disposable razor.

Today Wilkinson's still produces swords of the highest quality which are made from

The world's finest garden tools

Swordsmanship fashioned these tools. And Swordsmanship not only means the unique two hundred-year-old tradition of Wilkinson Sword: the proud tradition of putting the finest and most enduring edges on the finest steel. It also means we unceasingly search for and apply every technological advance and invention in metallurgy. This is why Wilkinson Sword are acknowledged to be the world's finest garden tools. They are fashioned with the same skill that has been the pride of generations of craftsmen: a skill enhanced by the ever-increasing advantages of space age techniques and space-age steel.

WILKINSON SWORD

IT'S THE NEW WAY IN SHAVING

commercial presentation, or to commemorate special events. The craft of the sword maker is perhaps best expressed in the Wilkinson Sword Armorial Bearings, granted to the company in its bicentennial year: *Semper Qualitas Suprema* – Always the Finest Quality.

FACING PAGE, TOP: *Corn razors, c. 1919*
FACING PAGE, BELOW RIGHT: *The T M C side-car combination, 1912*
LEFT: *Advertisement in Reader's Digest, 1969*
ABOVE: *Another Wilkinson diversification – garden tools*
BELOW: *Modern presentation swords*

its own specification specially smelted and roll-forged Sheffield high-carbon steel. Blades are hand-ground on 5-foot diameter carborundum wheels to the correct section and profile and then, after careful heat treatment, undergo stringent tests. Only when they have passed the scrutiny of the Master Cutler are they mirror-polished and acid etched with the required pattern and insignia. Finally, they are fitted with their hilt and, in some instances, with a scabbard. Each sword has a serial number which is entered in a record book, in the traditional manner. Not all Wilkinson swords are military ones, many being for civic regalia or

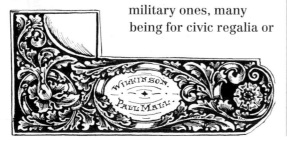

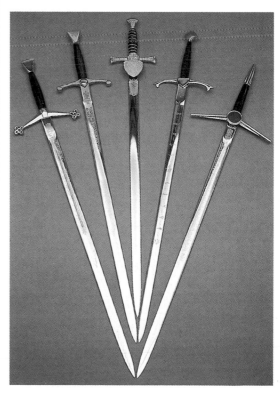

Wolsey

It is likely that Henry Wood, born 20 July 1707, learnt his skill as a stocking-frame operative from his father. Henry came from a modest background, but became a successful businessman, commencing trading in Leicester in 1744 as a hosier, and insuring his business stock and property, including three stocking-frames, for £200. From the beginning, he produced quality knitted goods, these having more elasticity than woven ones, moulding more to the shape of the body and being useful for close-fitting garments such as stockings, socks and vests, which were his original wares. However, knitted fabric requires considerable skill in production: the yarn must be even and well-twisted while the loops of thread should be the same size and successfully entwined.

In 1748, Henry Wood became a Freeman of the Borough of Leicester, a privilege signifying considerable personal and commercial achievement. That year, to gain further experience, he formed a partnership with Job Middleton, an established and self-made hosier. The partnership prospered and, in 1750, was joined by John Wightman, who brought additional capital. Henry now lived in Leicester's fashionable Friar Lane district, in a very desirable property with adjacent work-rooms and warehouses. These work-rooms were used by the partners to sort, dye and finish the high-quality goods which had been made by the frame-work knitters, who rented their stocking-frames from the company, and worked in their own homes, often in Leicester's surrounding villages.

Henry married Ann Blower in 1751; her mother was John Wightman's niece. However, by 1755, the partnerships had been dissolved and Henry was trading on his own account. As the business grew, Henry and Ann built an even grander house in Friar Lane, to make room for their growing family, and to provide further warehouses and residences for their workers. Sadly, Henry's health began to fail and Ann took an increasing lead in the running of the business; Henry died on 15 June 1768, aged

LEFT, AND FACING PAGE: *Stylish advertisements from the 1940s*
ABOVE: *Robert Walker*

sixty-one. The *Leicester Journal* reported he 'had acquired a very considerable fortune with great Industry and equal Reputation'. His wife was only forty-one and had a young family of seven children, aged between three and sixteen, to bring up. Unusually for his time, but with complete resolution, Henry had bequeathed all his 'stock in trade Debts and all other Goods Chattels and Personal Estate' directly to his widow as sole executrix. He specifically directed that Ann was to convert the estate into money and place the proceeds out 'upon good Public or Private Securities' for the benefit of herself and the children. However, contrary to her husband's directions, she took on his role within the company as sole proprietor and manager, a position she held for ten years. Such a decision was remarkable, showing her determination, knowledge and skill.

In 1777, Henry Wood's eldest son, Henry jnr, became a Freeman of the Borough of Leicester and entered into a partnership with his mother, being joined two years later by the next eldest son, Thomas. From then on the company traded, from Friar Lane, as 'Ann Wood & Sons', until she died in 1813, aged eighty-seven.

Holden's *Triennial Directory for 1805* states that the company was engaged in the manufacture of stockings, fancy hosiery, caps and spots (small cravats). Richard Warner Wood and Thomas Wood jnr joined their respective fathers, Henry and Thomas, in a new partnership and the range of goods was extended to include socks, sweaters and underwear. Thomas Wood jnr, when giving evidence to a government commission, stated that the company was principally engaged in the manufacture of hosiery and the majority of the production was sold to the 'Scotch' market. It may be that a business relationship existed between Ann Wood

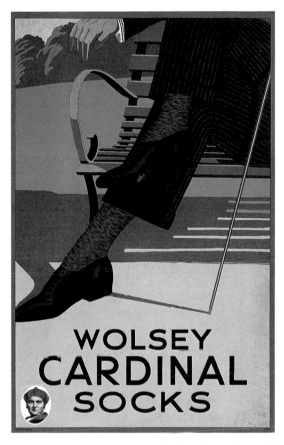

& Sons and the Glasgow wholesale and retail wool merchant and hosier, George Walker.

Through an irregularity in his father's will Robert Walker, George's son, was denied his inheritance and, at the age of sixteen, he travelled by stagecoach to Leicester to learn the trade he believed would return to him a position of affluence. After some years, he started working under contract for Ann Wood & Sons and, in 1842, he became a partner in the firm. In 1849, after seven successful years of partnership, Richard Wood retired and Robert Walker became the proprietor, changing the name to Robert Walker & Co. A man of strong faith and character, he took as his motto 'Weave Truth with Trust'.

Robert Walker was a talented and ambitious hosier who introduced new techniques into the Leicester hosiery trade. He pioneered the use of looser knitting techniques

WOLSEY
SPORTSMAN
Pullovers & Golf Hose

which gave garments a lighter weight, combined with an appearance of thickness and heaviness. This innovation endorsed the company's position as market leader.

As demand grew, he located all his knitting machines in the company's first steam-powered factory, built in the nearby village of Fleckney. In 1864, large new warehouses were built in Rutland Street, Leicester, being enlarged in 1876. By 1883, it was the largest hosiery company in the Leicester region and sales went to all parts of the world. Robert Walker died in 1883, during a visit to the Niagara Falls. His sons took control of the company and saw it move into the age of mechanization and new technology.

One most important discovery pioneered by the firm was the production of 'unshrinkable' woollens. To herald this achievement, an entirely new name was adopted for their products – on 12 October 1897, Theodore and Ralph Walker registered their new brand with the 'Wolsey' trademark. It was inspired by the powerful ecclesiastic and statesman, Cardinal Wolsey, who was buried in Leicester Abbey, only 400 yards from the Wolsey headquarters. On his death, Cardinal Wolsey was found to be wearing a woollen undergarment made by the Augustine Canons of the Abbey. The company stated: 'This trademark has a fuller meaning than the usual. It carries with it to the purchaser an assurance of superiority . . . has no equal in the world for lightness, durability and general excellence.'

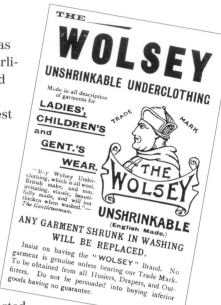

Wolsey was one of the earliest registered brands in Britain. Ernest Theodore Walker and Kenneth Walker, the two sons of the principals, in a display of commercial brilliance, suggested that the firm ought to spend not less than £10,000 every year on advertising campaigns – at this point, the two had not yet joined the company and had to ask their respective mothers to persuade their fathers to consider the project. The suggestion was adopted and Wolsey initiated significant brand advertising, the first appearing in the *Drapers Record* in 1898.

When Edward VII acceded to the throne, there grew a great interest in sporting activities. The company lost no opportunity in publicizing that both Captain Scott's and Ernest Shackleton's expeditions to the North and South Poles were wearing Wolsey underwear to protect them from the hostile environment.

Between 1885 and 1900, golf was experiencing a boom time. Ernest T Walker, proud of his Scottish heritage, and with a strong love of golf, became the driving force for Wolsey's expansion into sportswear, this being marketed under the name 'Sportsman'.

In 1910, a new factory was opened at Abbey Meadows. They supplied at least 18 million articles for the troops, ranging from underwear, to jerseys and scarves. Wolsey

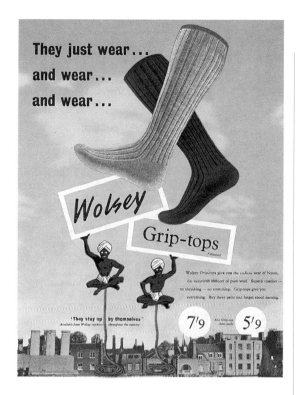

They just wear...
and wear...
and wear...

Wolsey

Grip-tops

also developed special stump mitts and socks for amputees injured in the fighting.

In 1919, Robert Walker & Sons ceased to market through wholesalers and began to supply retailers direct. The company amalgamated with W Tyler & Sons in 1920 and, following this merger, a public company was formed which adopted the title of Wolsey Limited, reflecting the strength of the brand name's reputation.

During the 1920s, Wolsey manufactured a very wide range of products from swimsuits to golf clothes, blouses and shirts, and suits, pullovers and dresses. They made sportscoats for men and women in wool, alpaca, cashmere and rayon, and also many jerseys for boys and girls. The late 1920s and early 1930s, however, brought difficult years in the economic recession – at one point Wolsey was losing £20,000 a week. Still they continued to trade strongly overseas and, in 1932, employed fifty-six overseas agents, representing fifty-eight countries. Famous adver-

tising slogans were to follow, such as 'miles more wear' being promised from silk stockings – items selected by the Royal Household for the footmen at Buckingham Palace. In 1935, Wolsey was appointed a Royal Warrant holder as Hosiery Manufacturers to His Majesty King George V.

Ernest T Walker was the last Walker to chair the company. He died in 1949 and was succeeded by Arthur Leslie Miller, who had joined the company as a salesman. When, in the 1950s and 1960s, chain stores grew in number and importance, Miller firmly rejected any demands to supply non-branded items, ensuring the survival of the Wolsey brand.

In 1967, after Arthur Miller's retirement, Wolsey became part of Courtaulds Textiles Group, one of the largest textile companies in Europe. In 1972, Wolsey became the first company in the world to have the Woolblendmark, which provides instore identification for garments made from wool-rich blends and which meet standards of performance and wool content.

you've got to come to Britain

for socks like

In 1996, following a management buyout, Wolsey is once again an independent company, seeking to retain and develop those standards for which it has been known for so long.

Wolsey

FACING PAGE, TOP LEFT:
Advertising sportswear
FACING PAGE, TOP RIGHT:
Advertisement in Windsor
Magazine, *1899*
ABOVE LEFT: *Advertisement
from 1956*
RIGHT: *Advertisement in*
Illustrated, *1953*

YARDLEY

LONDON

In the reign of Charles I a young man named Yardley paid the monarch a large sum for a concession to manufacture soap for the whole of London. Many of the details of the deal were lost in the Fire of London, but we do know that he used lavender to perfume his soap, a fragrance for which the House of Yardley is still famous.

In the eighteenth century, a descendant, William Yardley, travelled to London, taking with him a small fortune and lots of ambition. There, he joined a friend named Beedal who taught him enough to start on his own as a sword, spur and buckle maker. Within six weeks of Beedal's death, in 1780, Yardley married his widow. They had seven children, including a

daughter called Hermina. In 1801, Hermina married William Cleaver, heir to an important soap and perfumery business, founded by his father in 1770 in the City of London.

Wigs for men had gone out of fashion and they often dressed their own hair with lavish amounts of oils and dressings such as bear's grease. Perfumes were still very simple, mainly produced by macerating flowers and distilling them in water, and the favourite flower used was lavender. Lip salves, face powders and liquid rouges were all in general use, the rouge being applied with a small sponge over a base of bear's grease.

It was fashionable to be extravagant at

ABOVE LEFT: *William Yardley*
ABOVE: *Early enamel lid*
LEFT: *Flower sellers*
FACING PAGE, BELOW LEFT AND TOP RIGHT: *Advertisements in* Scottish Field, *1954*

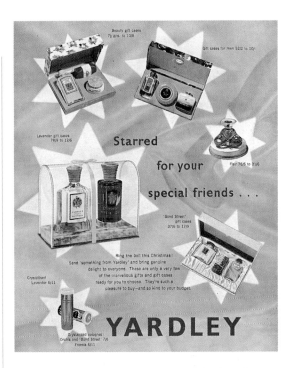

the gaming tables and fortunes were frequently won or lost; this was the tragedy which befell William Cleaver and Hermina. Coutts Bank had advanced William £2,000, on the security of the soap and perfumery business, but now he could not repay the loan. As William Yardley had stood as guarantor, he had to pay the debt, and so he took over the Cleaver business.

William Yardley continued as a sword-cutler in Bloomsbury, but moved the lavender, cosmetics and soap business next door to his own sword business. On his death in 1824, he left the soap and cosmetics business to his younger son Charles, who had little interest in it, being more interested in helping Sir Robert Peel in the formation of the British police force. Charles Yardley placed his own son in the business, and also appointed a partner, the firm becoming

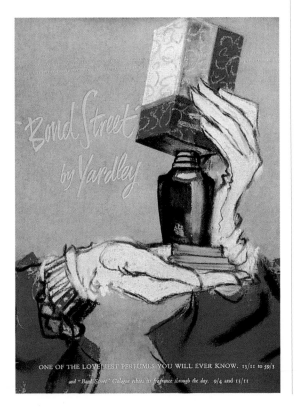

ONE OF THE LOVELIEST PERFUMES YOU WILL EVER KNOW. 13/11 to 59/3
and "Bond Street" Cologne echoes its fragrance through the day. 9/4 and 13/11

Yardley & Statham. They exhibited at the Great Exhibition of 1851. Included in the display was a sample cake of Old Brown Windsor soap, which carried an embossed representation of Windsor Castle; this is still preserved at Yardley House.

When Statham died, Robert Blake Yardley was too young to take over and Thomas Exton Gardner was brought in as a partner. At this point, the company grew quickly, exporting twenty-two varieties of Yardley soap to the United States in 1879. The following year, Yardley & Co Ltd was formed with capital of £172,000, but the next few years were difficult ones for the company, and by 1899 the future of the firm looked doubtful.

When Thomas Gardner's sons entered the business, they quickly took positions of responsibility, Thornton Gardner becoming Managing Director and Richard Company Secretary. They decided that, if the firm was to grow on a national and international basis, they must trade exclusively under the name of Yardley and not make cakes of soap bearing the names of individual chemists.

New premises were established in Carpenters Road at Stratford, London. Overseas sales were established in Sydney, Australia, and, in 1910, a major decision was taken to open a fashionable London centre at 8 New Bond Street.

Ten years earlier Yardley was hardly known to the general public, but now, with its presence in New Bond Street and effective publicity, it had become a nationally known name. In 1913, the firm adopted Francis Wheatley's 'Flower Sellers Group', one of fourteen paintings in the 'Cries of London' series, as its trademark for all its lavender products.

After the First World War, Yardley, already the largest manufacturer of lavender-based cosmetics, advertised extensively to stimulate demand for its products. It also sent John H Seager, a young chemist, round the world to study and develop a strain of lavender, which was grown exclusively for Yardley in Norfolk.

In the 1930s, spirit duty for lavender was lifted and turnover doubled. In 1933, the Yardley poster of that period was voted 'Poster of the Year' at the Advertisers' Convention.

In the 1950s, girls aged from about fourteen were starting to use make-up; that period also saw the introduction of a range of toiletries for men, the Yardley 'Y' Range.

To give the company the resources to embark on research and development programmes, it became part of British-American Tobacco, which, in 1970, co-ordinated its cosmetic interests in British American Cosmetics.

For fifty-five years, Yardley traded from 33 Old Bond Street, but, in 1989, the firm moved to premises in Holborn before it became the Yardley Lentheric Group and moved to Camberley.

In 1993, the head office moved to the factory site at Basildon, Essex and reverted to the name Yardley of London. It is now owned by Wasserstein Perella, investment bankers based in New York.

ABOVE AND BELOW: *Two of today's Yardley products*